W9-DCT-327

Religion and Philosophy

AN
ALDUS
BOOK

Worship is transcendent wonder.

Thomas Carlyle (1795–1881)

Philosophy is the product of wonder. The effort after the general characterization of the world around us is the romance of human thought.

Alfred North Whitehead (1861–1947)

CURTIS INTERNATIONAL/LIBRARY OF KNOWLEDGE

RELIGION AND PHILOSOPHY

AN ALDUS BOOK

Fresco of St. Thomas Aquinas as the focus of an allegory on learning. All medieval learning and teaching came directly from the Church, so religious references were common in works of art and literature.

CURTIS BOOKS
A division of
The Curtis Publishing Company
Philadelphia • New York

13th-century maze laid out in colored marble on the floor of Chartres Cathedral in France.

Printed in Germany by Mohndruck, Gütersloh.
Library of Congress Catalog No. 68-26186.

CONTENTS

Religion probably developed from man's conviction that there are forces more powerful than himself on which his life depends. Gradually a comprehensive system of ideas concerning the nature of the world evolved. Philosophy emerged from these conjectures. The questions asked by both philosophers and theologians have changed over the centuries, but both have consistently struggled to define the nature of the world and man's role in it.

EARLY RELIGION

The origins and patterns of early religion can only be guessed at on the basis of rather scanty archaeological evidence and observation of contemporary primitive societies. Historical knowledge of Mediterranean and western Asian civilizations dates from the fourth millennium B.C. Polytheism was the general form of belief. The emergence of cults associated with particular gods anticipated the development of the major historical religions.

From earliest times man has been preoccupied with the mystery of death and what lay beyond it, questions which led his mind into the realms of the supernatural. Christianity sprang from such beginnings, and pictures of the Crucifixion—a visible reminder of the promised life after death—have always been popular.

The Beginnings of Religion

Scholars do not know exactly what the beginnings of religion were. However, studying the habits and objects of prehistoric men, and the primitive cultures of our own time, suggests that men have generally felt compelled to look beyond themselves to forces which need some explanation other than practical cause and effect. Modern primitive societies do not specifically explain any religions other than their own, but they provide an instructive parallel with prehistoric beliefs and worship.

Two basic puzzles of human existence seem to have stimulated early men to postulate and respect forces beyond the tangible world around them: death and the vagaries of crops and game. There is definite evidence of Stone Age men's interest in the problem of death. The Neanderthalers, who lived from 100,000 to 25,000 years ago, buried their dead with ceremony, putting flint instruments in the graves. The later Cro-Magnon men surrounded their dead with ornaments, weapons and food and smeared ocher, a red, blood-like coloring, on the bodies. They may well have believed in an afterlife, given the care with which the dead were buried.

Although the annual cycle of plant life is fairly regular, the supply of game to a hunting people is more variable. The Cro-Magnon men possessed highly-developed artistic skills, which scholars are certain were used not primarily for decoration but for religious or magical purposes. The animals painted on the walls of deep caves in northern Spain and southern France are often depicted with spears or darts in them. It seems clear that the artists were trying to stimulate some superhuman force to provide game and make it vulnerable. Men believed that there was such a force and that they could somehow communicate with it.

The belief that man can sense awesome and uncanny forces (a phenomenon called numinism, from the Latin *numen*, a spirit) lies at the root of all known religions. And it seems probable that numinous experiences, coinciding with various aspects of nature and their changes, gave early men a belief in supernatural cause and effect. For instance, the force that brings new life and fresh growth in the spring can be encouraged not to fail by honoring it with fertility rites.

Early religions attached spiritual importance to animals and plants as well. Some Australian aborigines, like many American Indian tribes, identify families and clans with particular animals and plants, a practice known as totemism. Respect for the animal ensures its survival and that of the tribe. Most early religions lacking any form of totem system personified their beliefs in particular nature spirits or gave them identifying names or qualities. Often these spirits developed into a range of different gods to worship for different things (polytheism), and in some cases a superior god was assumed to exist above them.

There are no perfect definitions of what religion is, but it may be described as an attempt to discover, define and control (or submit advantageously to) causes of things that cannot be explained in material terms; to find some sense in death; to understand and control the apparently accidental good fortune of some men and the bad luck of others; and to ensure that the earth continues to provide food. Twentieth-century science provides some of the meteorological and agricultural answers that primitive men lacked, but in primitive terms much of early religion seems quite reasonable. An accident or coincidence that produces a desired effect—like a drought broken the day after a spontaneous dance—can be repeated and turned into a ritual to make it happen again. Or a tribal chieftain's death on the day his son shoots a rabbit for the first time can lead to a ban on any member of the tribe attacking a rabbit, making it *taboo*.

As early religions developed into systems with a body of ritual, local history and myth often became involved with religious lore; for the origin of the world and man's place in it were as puzzling as death. Explanations of these questions vary enormously, but they are still basic to modern religion. Although science can explain most phenomena of the here and now, men everywhere still seek hope beyond the few decades of individual existence.

Above: aerial photo reveals traces of an Iron-Age burial ground at Lindholm in Denmark. Since the Stone Age, man has buried the dead with care, showing his concern for a possible life after death. Right: Eskimo mask represents a swan and has a magical significance in whale-hunting. By wearing such a mask, the hunter believes he actually becomes an animal (the swan) and is thus able to lure his prey (the whale) toward him.

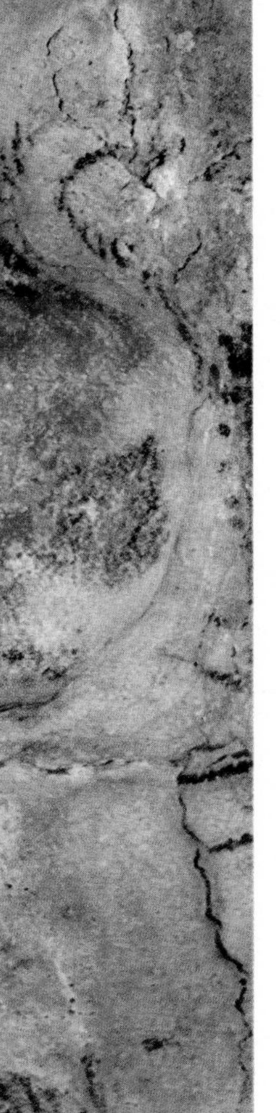

The religious beliefs and customs of modern primitive societies provide a parallel with those of prehistoric man, who used religion in an effort to control his environment. Left: prehistoric cave painting in Altamira, Spain. Hunting tribes painted animals stuck with spears in the hope that the gods would send game. Right: in the Congo today the rainmaker sways in a ritual dance, calling on the gods to send the rain so desperately needed to water the pastureland for his tribe's cattle.

Egyptian Religion

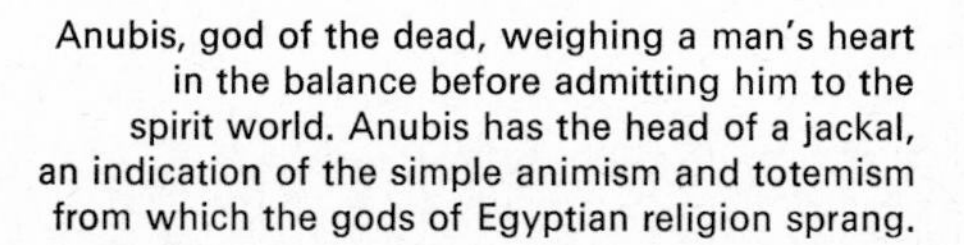

Anubis, god of the dead, weighing a man's heart in the balance before admitting him to the spirit world. Anubis has the head of a jackal, an indication of the simple animism and totemism from which the gods of Egyptian religion sprang.

As villages along the Nile developed into communities and were unified—usually by one community conquering and absorbing another—the religion of ancient Egypt developed from simple spirit-worship and totemism into a highly organized polytheism. By 2900 B.C. Egypt was one kingdom, and the various animal guardians of previously isolated villages had been amalgamated into a single religious system.

The chief features of Egyptian gods were their dual or treble natures, often combining animal, human and superhuman characteristics. For example, Anubis, the guardian and guide of the dead in the underworld, was depicted with a jackal's head. Thoth, the god of learning, had the head of an ibis (a stork-like bird). The most powerful and important gods were often fusions of gods who had been worshiped in separate villages earlier. The god of the sun and chief of the Egyptian divine hierarchy was Ra—for the sun was all-important to an agricultural society. He incorporated aspects of earlier gods: Aton, the sun god and father; and Horus, the falcon god and avenger, lord of the upper world, often the son of the Sun. As the son of Osiris and Isis (brother and sister monarchs of the Nile), and grandson of Get the earth god and Nut the sky goddess, Horus played an important part in Egyptian religious myth. His uncle and great enemy was Seth, lord of darkness and the underworld, depicted as part man, part greyhound.

The rising sun, Khepera, was identified with the dung beetle, which rolls its eggs in a huge ball of dung like the round sun moving across the sky. The beetle, or scarab, became symbolic of the sun. Ra, the life-giving sun, was also the source of the ruler's power; and the pharaohs assumed the title "Son of Ra" to affirm their godlike status and divine right to rule.

In addition to the political and religious stability of a kingdom whose ruler is officially accepted as an intermediary between heaven and earth, the chief feature of ancient Egyptian religion was its elaborate and spectacular cult of the dead. As Osiris was the son of earth and sky and the god of vegetation, and as the pharaohs were held to be of divine descent, it was important to ensure their immortality in order to guarantee the fertility of the realm. Beliefs about the afterlife were complex; different at different times as to what the soul was and how to preserve it; but life after death was accepted as certain. To retain a home for the various shadowy aspects of the soul, the body had to be preserved; and elaborate mummification techniques developed. The mummies were surrounded with food, clothing, games and great treasures—and models of their

The Egyptian ruler Amenhotep IV (14th century B.C.), who tried to substitute monotheism for the rivalries of the old cults and dogmas. He forbade the worship of all gods except Aton, the sun god, and changed his own name to Ikhnaton, meaning "Glory of Aton."

Right: scarab amulet (30 B.C) inscribed with a prayer to the gods. After death, preservation of the corpse was vital to the immortality of the soul, so before burial the heart was often removed and such an amulet put in its place to protect the body from dangers like decay and tomb robbers. In time, the living also came to wear protective amulets to ensure divine favor.

Below: dung beetle pushing the huge ball of dung that contains its eggs. It is easy to see how the Egyptians associated this with the round sun moving across the sky; and the beetle, or scarab, became a sacred symbol of the sun god Khepera.

women and servants. At first, only the families of the pharaohs were considered immortal and entombed in such splendor, but gradually everyone who could afford it arranged for extravagant burial.

After death, the soul was judged by Osiris, who admitted the good soul into his realm (or as some cults believed, to unity with the sun). The bad soul was condemned to a kind of hell or to be eaten by the Devourer, who had a crocodile's head, lion's forequarters and hindquarters of a hippopotamus.

Although for centuries priests in different parts of Egypt adhered to cults of one god or another and preached different schemes for the soul after death, one pharaoh made a distinguished attempt toward monotheism. Amenhotep IV ruled in the 14th century B.C. Changing his name to Ikhnaton (Glory of Aton), he tried to substitute the worship of one god, Aton, the solar disk, for the rivalries of different cults. But the powerful priests resisted, and his successor, Tutenkhamon, returned to polytheism.

The complexities of Egyptian religion did not survive several centuries of invasions, however. By the third century A.D. most of Egypt had become Christian.

The Religion of Mesopotamia

Above: clay model of a sheep's liver (about 1700 B.C.) marked to guide priests, who used animals' organs to determine the will of the gods.

Between the Tigris and Euphrates rivers in Mesopotamia, the powerful Sumerian cities and kingdoms arose. They fought among themselves for dominance and later were absorbed first by Semitic and then by Persian kingdoms. During the 3,000 years before the time of Christ, the peoples of this area worshiped a number of different gods. With political amalgamation, the Sumerian pantheon came to include almost 4,000 different deities, most representing aspects of nature.

Originally, six gods—identified with the great cities of the area—were predominant: Anu, the god of heaven; Enlil, the air god; Sin, the moon god; Babar (or Shamash), the sun god; Ea (or Enki), the water god and Nintud, the mother goddess. The home cities of these gods permitted the cults of the others as well, and sanctuaries for lesser deities. At different periods the status of the gods varied, and some lesser deities ultimately became more important than the six gods.

Perhaps the goddess most universally worshiped was Ishtar (or Astarte), the Semitic goddess of fertility, who took on many aspects of Nintud and other mother goddesses. As the planet Venus, she was queen of the heavens, and Ishtar-worship endured and spread. She figures in Hebrew mythology and was combined with the Egyptian goddess Isis in the later Hellenistic period.

The god Marduk achieved at least equal prominence when his city, Babylon, became predominant in the second millennium B.C. as the capital of an empire extending to the Persian Gulf. He assumed Ea's wisdom and Enlil's power. After defeating the dragon of chaos, Tiamat, he became king of the gods and created man. Like Marduk's ascendancy, other religious developments were the direct results of political change linked to changes in the status of the area's cities, states and empires.

The Sumerians, Babylonians and Assyrians amassed a great body of myths about their gods and frequently altered the names of heroes to glorify the predominant god or gods of a particular period. The original great flood story is Sumerian. Told in the epic of *Gilgamesh* (which relates the journeys of the ruler of Erech to the waters of death and back), it closely parallels the biblical story of the ark, the flood and the dove. Other stories in the Gilgamesh epic reinforce the importance of life in this world, rather than an all-important afterlife.

Although the Mesopotamians appear to have believed in some kind of life after death, the practices of their religion concentrated on what the gods

Tablet from the epic of Gilgamesh. The hero sets out to find the secret of immortality but returns without it. Concerned with life in this world, the Babylonians were resigned to physical death.

could do to increase the blessings of life on earth. Their priests were well-educated and highly organized. Clay tablets found by archaeologists confirm that Mesopotamian temples were run like large corporations, as legal entities with efficient accounting and often very large landholdings. Education was in the hands of the priests, who taught reading, writing and arithmetic. A great part of their duties included divination—learning the will of the gods from the examination of the liver of a freshly-slaughtered sheep, or through astrology. Because they attempted to discover the gods' will by examining the behavior of heavenly bodies, recording the movement of the stars and planets known to them, they prepared the way for later scientific astronomy.

Another order of priests specialized in interpreting dreams and unusual events—again to learn what personal and political developments the gods held in store for the people and the state. They were paid by the faithful for sacrifices and long incantations and liturgies to influence the gods by confessing unworthiness, and even casting spells.

Although the changing emphases of Mesopotamian religion may seem inconsistent now, the flexibility made it possible to adapt smoothly to political change—until the Persians captured Babylon in A.D. 539 and Mesopotamian religion passed into history.

Above: ziggurat at Ur in Iraq. This massive structure, towering over its surrounding compound, formed the focal point of a Babylonian temple, which was run by highly-organized priests who were the educators and spiritual guides of the community.

Below: worshiper of Ishtar, goddess of fertility (temple statue of third millennium B.C.). Ishtar played an important part in the spring festival in Babylon when she was said to rescue her son, the vegetation god Tammuz, from the kingdom of the dead. His return and marriage to her annually restored fertility to the land.

The Mother Goddess and the Sky God

Two observations about life and its origins pervaded early beliefs and retain a place in many modern religions as well. The first is that the sun in the sky gives warmth and light and, like the rain which falls from the same heaven, is vital for the growth and survival of all living things. The second is that mothers give birth to babies. With a thousand different names and attributes, mother goddesses have been worshiped as life-givers all over the world. There is evidence that primitive peoples, who may not have understood the father's role in reproduction very well, involved themselves in fertility cults centered on females as the source of life. Certainly, archaeologists have found a wide range of prehistoric figures of women with exaggerated breasts and bellies.

The mother goddess, as the giver of life, is associated with the cycle of nature, and the changing seasons. She often has a special relationship to animals, like the Greek goddess Artemis, at once

Above: two clay figures of the mother goddess, from Crete (left) and India (right). Besides her role of ensuring fertility, she sometimes had a special association with animals. The Cretan goddess has snakes twining round her arms, symbols of the gods of the hearth—she was a protectress of the home as well.

Above: the Venus of Laussel, rock carving (about 15,000–10,000 B.C.), thought to be associated with a fertility cult, is probably one of the earliest known representations of the mother goddess. Right: another fertility figure from Asia Minor (about 2500 B.C.).

Right: a Theban sarcophagus (second century A.D.) contains a portrait of the Egyptian sky goddess, Nut. The wife of Geb and mother of Isis and Osiris, Nut personified the heavenly vault; it was believed that she swallowed the sun every night and gave birth to it again each morning.

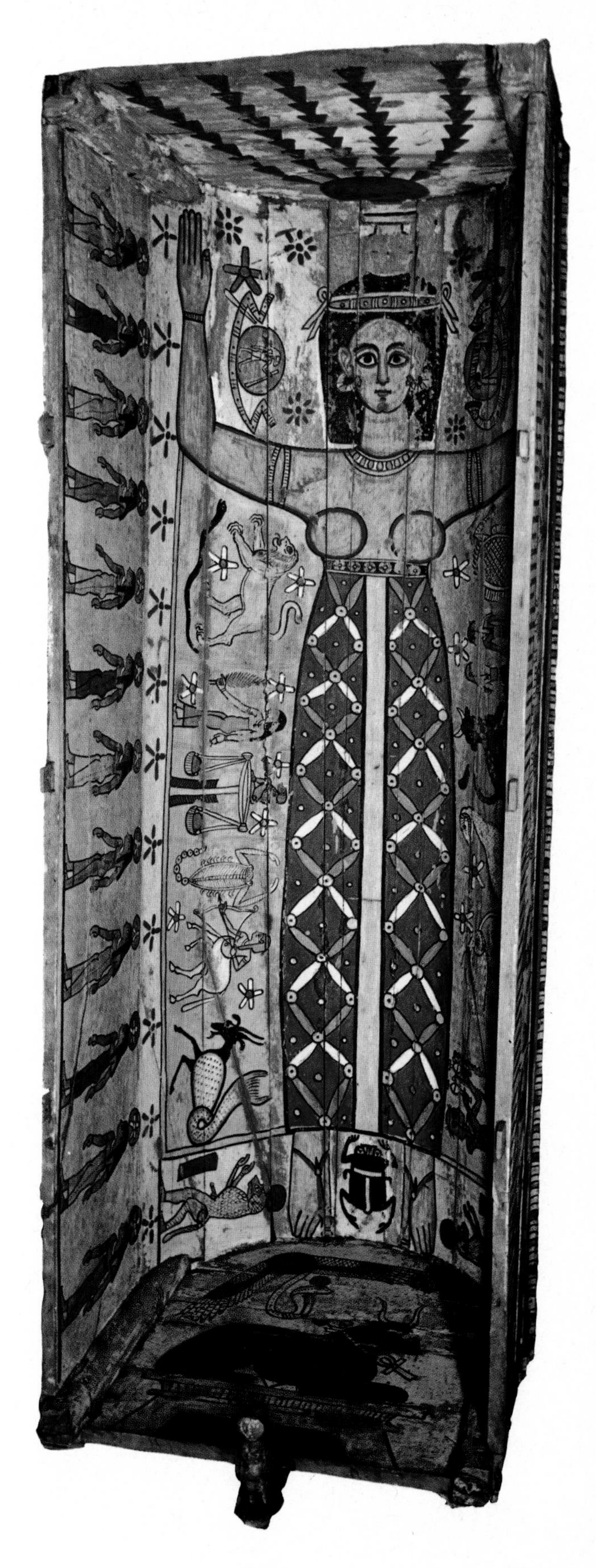

huntress and patroness of wild beasts. Ishtar in Mesopotamia and Isis in Egypt filled roles as mother goddesses, and their sons had special importance, undergoing the death and resurrection which symbolizes the death of plants and their rebirth in the spring. The Cretan mother goddess of the Minoan period (about 3000–1100 B.C.) combined several roles. She was a lady of the animals and also a mistress of the underworld. She was often depicted grasping snakes in her hand. Snakes receive special reverence as household spirits in some parts of the world, and some mother goddesses are domestic protectresses as well.

In Greek and Roman religion, several goddesses shared aspects of the mother goddess. In Eastern religions, the mothers of the great sages are often given high importance. In faiths with only one god (monotheism, like Judaism, Islam and Christianity), she appears to be missing—but many Roman Catholics venerate Mary. Although subordinate to the divinity of God and Jesus Christ, she is prayed to both as the mother of Jesus and as the intercessor between human beings and God.

The other important figure, the sky god, appears in equal variety. Often he is the superior figure in a whole pantheon of gods and goddesses, lawgiver to the universe and ruler of the sun deities. Ordinary human affairs are served by lesser divinities. A sky god preceded the Egyptian cult of the sun, and the Sumerians divided his attributes between two gods, Anu and Enlil. The chief gods of Greece and Rome, Zeus and Jupiter, are identified with the sky; both names are derived from the Indo-European Dyaus Pitar (sky father). Yahweh, who gave the Ten Commandments to Moses on Mount Sinai, also had some attributes of the sky god.

When they invaded India from the northwest in the second millennium B.C., the Indo-Europeans had several major gods. In addition to Dyaus, Indra was very important. God of battle and rain and thunder, he was the son of Dyaus and the earth goddess. Varuna, as lord of heaven, was the guardian of *rta* (related to the word "right"), the basic cosmic law which governs the entire universe, nature as well as man. (A variation of Varuna's name remains in the Greek Uranus, Heaven.) Although Varuna was never worshiped as the only god, his identification with the moral principle represented the Indo-Europeans' closest approach to monotheism.

Left: the treasury of Atreus at Delphi, which lies to the north of Chalcis in Euboea, Greece. Statesmen and ordinary people from every part of the Greek peninsula came to Delphi to consult the famous oracle whose predictions were accepted by these pilgrims as coming straight from the gods themselves. The Pythian festivals, held regularly at Delphi, included recitals of music and poetry as well as contests in athletics. By 600 B.C., Delphi had become the political and cultural center of the loose union of Greek city-states which existed at that time.

The Gods of Greece

Like that of the Sumerians, the Greek pantheon developed as a fusion of the gods worshiped by immigrants and invaders in various parts of the Greek peninsula and the islands near it. The Cretans of the Minoan period had a fertility cult centered on a mother goddess. The Dorians, Indo-European invaders from the north, then brought their gods to Greece: Dyaus Pitar, the sky father, whom the Greeks called Zeus; Demeter, the earth mother and Hestia, goddess of the hearth. The local nature gods of mainland Greece, a country of mountains and isolated valleys, shared characteristics of the Cretan and Dorian gods.

By the time of the Homeric epics (about ninth century B.C.), Zeus and his dozens of wives and divine and heroic offspring were recognized in one form or another throughout the Greek city-states. In practice, they were venerated in different ways. Zeus, for example, was generally the chief god and rainmaker. In some places he was important as a fertility god, in others as a god of the underworld, and as the local nature god of many mountaintops all over Greece.

Hera was queen of the gods and goddess of marriage; Athena, the wise virgin goddess of Athens and protectress of the arts; Hermes, the messenger; Aphrodite, the goddess of love. Persephone (daughter of the earth goddess Demeter) returned from the underworld each spring with new life. Artemis was goddess of the hunt; and her brother Apollo was the divinely handsome god of youth, music and poetry. Apollo's oracle at Delphi,

In this Greek vase painting Zeus sends an eagle to devour Prometheus' liver to punish him for stealing the secret of fire and giving it to man.

where a priestess (intoxicated by vapors rising from a vent in the ground) made mysterious predictions, was second in importance only to the oracles of Zeus.

The Homeric pantheon was highly sophisticated. The gods were no longer aspects of nature or even personifications of them. They were anthropomorphic—with human shape and attributes—immortal creatures in charge of various divisions and functions of nature and human activity. Their behavior, fights and love affairs were very human—and the Greek sculptors portrayed them as realistic, if somewhat idealized, human beings. Unlike some early cultures, the Greeks did not fear their gods.

The classical age of Greece produced a formal and aristocratic pattern of worship. Western drama originated in the dialogues of religious festivals, probably first in the spring celebrations of death and rebirth. The advice given by the priestess at the Delphic oracle clearly influenced political decisions; but in general the community, rather than the priesthood, was predominant. The dignified and formal religious festivals became official occasions, civic ceremonies that lacked any personal appeal. The stately temples built to house the shrines of gods like Zeus and Athena are among history's finest examples of architecture and have been copied in the West for centuries. Statues of the gods have a universal respect and appeal, not for their religious significance, but for their sheer beauty and harmony. And the Greek drama that developed out of earlier religious ceremony produced playwrights like Aeschylus, Sophocles and Euripides, who used the gods and traditional myths as a framework for portraying human character and action.

Apollo pursues Hercules, who had seized the sacred tripod from the shrine of the Delphic oracle; its priestess had censured him for murdering a guest and refused to tell him how to be rid of evil dreams. Zeus halted them with a thunderbolt, ordering them to be reconciled. The quarrels of the gods often had a human quality.

The very sophistication of Olympian religion reduced worship to an empty pattern for many people. Its lack of strong ethical and intellectual content led the educated classes to the rationalist philosophies which developed alongside it, for their more plausible speculations about the world and man, and how human beings ought to behave. Others turned to mystery cults offering personal involvement.

King Aegeus of Athens consults the oracle at Delphi, in this painting on a Greek bowl (fifth century B.C.). The priestess, intoxicated by the vapors rising from a vent in the ground, gave answers to questions on religious, ethical and political matters in an enigmatic manner.

Above: Demeter and her daughter Persephone, the corn maiden (part of the Elgin Marbles). Based on the myth of Demeter's search for Persephone and her conditional release from Hades, the Eleusinian mysteries celebrated the annual death and rebirth of grain.

Mystery Religions in Greece

The chief appeal of mystery cults was their privacy and the personal satisfaction they gave their adherents. They were called mysteries because their ritual sites were kept secret except, of course, to initiates. Although the cults varied in emphasis and style, the initiation processes were similar. Guided by a *hierophant* (one who reveals holy things) the candidates were first purified (by being washed, or dipped in the sea or a sacred stream, for example). Then they were instructed in the secret knowledge of the cult and permitted to view its sacred objects. The viewing was usually followed by a dramatic presentation and the crowning or wreathing of the candidates. They were then full-fledged initiates, privileged to take part in the cult's ceremonies, processions and sacred revels. It was thus a very personal religion, and the actual rites afforded initiates the kind of excitement that made them believe they were infused with the spirit of the god.

The Eleusinian mysteries, so called because they were celebrated at a place called Eleusis near Athens, were the oldest and most restrained. They were dedicated to the goddess of agriculture, Demeter. In the myth, Demeter's daughter, Persephone, disappears to the underworld, and after a long and sorrowful search, Demeter finds her and tries to bring her back. But Hades, the king of the underworld, tricks Persephone into staying there as his queen for one third of the year. As the grain maiden, Persephone returns to earth each spring. The solemn Eleusinian rituals included night-long vigils and processions in the autumn in imitation of Demeter's search for her daughter. There were also ritual dramas, enacted chiefly by women, to symbolize the death and rebirth of grain, a combination of concerns for agriculture and a future life.

A great many gods attracted mystery cults, but the most important were the Eleusinian mysteries and the wilder cults of Dionysus and Orpheus.

Dionysus, god of wine (and as such also associated with Demeter and the Eleusinian cult), was never quite as thoroughly assimilated into the Olympic pantheon as most of the other gods. The wildness of his cult was in direct contrast to the decorous formality of the mainstream of Greek religion.

As the god of wine, Dionysus was celebrated with ritual intoxication, which encouraged believers to feel that the god took possession of them. His mythical fortunes were celebrated in the rites: As the son of Zeus and Semele, Dionysus was killed and eaten by the Titans, enemies of the Olympians. Zeus retaliated by burning up the Titans with his thunderbolts, and the human race formed from their ashes is thus composed of both evil and good. The Dionysian mysteries included eating the flesh of a sacred kid or bull, identified with Dionysus in a kind of sacred communion imitating his death. His celebrants included the *maenads*, rushing and raging in wild excitement in the frenzied rites which brought a sacramental union with the god.

The cult of Orpheus, patron of music and a priest of Dionysus who was torn to pieces by maenads, shared many features with the Dionysian mysteries. However, it developed a distinctly ethical content. Believing that the body was imprisoning the soul, the Orphics cultivated moral purity to release the soul from its series of reincarnations, and regarded eating the sacred animal flesh as a means of strengthening the divine element within themselves. Their emphasis on moral asceticism and purity in this world greatly influenced contemporary Greek philosophers.

Above: Dionysus, surrounded by maenads, or worshipers, dancing in the frenzied manner characteristic of the cult of the god of wine. (Greek vase painting of 500 B.C.) Euripides illustrated the fatal excesses of some of these devotees in his tragedy, the *Bacchae*.

As an ecstatic outlet for emotional needs and a meaningful guide to behavior, the mysteries offset the impersonal official religion. Their personal impact outlasted belief in the gods of Olympus (the Eleusinian mysteries were brought to an end only when Alaric the Goth destroyed the temple at Eleusis in the fourth century) and attracted followers elsewhere. Romans, including some emperors, also became initiates.

This painting of Christ as Orpheus, the good shepherd, comes from the Roman catacombs (A.D. 300). As Orpheus tamed animals with his lyre, so the Orphics attempted to subdue or "tame" the bestial part of their own natures, seeking moral purity and release from the cycle of death and rebirth.

Roman Religion

In common with the religion of the Greeks, Roman religion was highly formalized and made up of a number of different strands. The ancient Roman religion was very close to magic; and, although its spirits were scrupulously venerated, they were largely formless—numina with mysterious magical powers. Although they often had quite clear functions and names, they lacked personality and sometimes even a precise sex. These impersonal gods existed merely as influences of natural phenomena, spirits of streams and groves and human concerns and activities. There were no pictures or statues and no myths about them. Only their function was important, and the rituals of propitiation were complex.

Priests and followers paid close attention to taboos, charms, incantations and the reading of omens—an elaborate systematization to keep believers on good terms with spirits whose personalities were as imprecise as their functions were specific. Farmers turned to Saturn for sowing and Ceres for the growth of grain. Flora presided over flowers, Faunus over the woods. Spirits called *Lares* were in control of the sown fields and later came to be the guardians of the household. *Penates* preserved the food in the household cupboard. Two other household gods were equally vital: Janus guarded the door, and Vesta the hearth. Above them all, Jupiter, the great sky father, produced sun and rain.

Roman gods were worshiped more in deed than in thought. The great number of ceremonies and festivals honoring them were matter-of-fact and specific. The performance of rituals and incantations had something of the nature of a legal contract; if the participants performed correctly, the gods were believed to be obligated to grant favor or lose their homage. Priests were vital and powerful, since they were the guardians and instructors of correct ceremonies, especially in the state rituals.

The numerous gods of the Roman state were honored on at least 104 days of the year with precise sacrifices and ceremonies. Jupiter, director of human affairs, guardian of law, and later the special defender of Rome, was chief among them. Mars, originally a protector from inimical forces generally, gradually became the powerful war god of imperial Rome. Janus and Vesta were invoked and honored at the beginning and end of state ceremonies.

By the eighth century B.C., the Latins of western central Italy found themselves between the Etruscans (who are believed to have invaded from the eastern Mediterranean) in the north and Greek colonists in the south. Etruscan and Greek association with the Latins in peace and war contributed to the subsequent character of Roman religion. The Etruscans introduced new gods (Minerva, goddess of wisdom and patroness of art and trade, was probably Etruscan) and organized family groupings among the new and old deities. Their chief innovation was personalizing the Romans' shadowy numina. In the temple of Jupiter on Rome's Capitoline hill they set statues of Jupiter, Juno and Minerva, and in general gave gods bodies and faces.

The Greek influence also contributed to giving human form to the Roman spirits. Roman gods came to be identified with Greek counterparts:

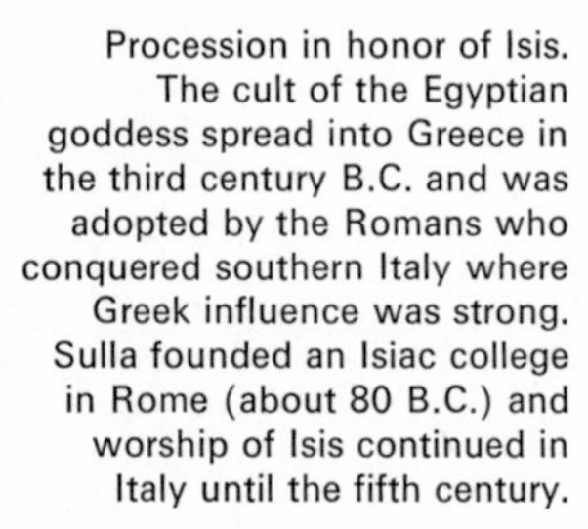

Procession in honor of Isis. The cult of the Egyptian goddess spread into Greece in the third century B.C. and was adopted by the Romans who conquered southern Italy where Greek influence was strong. Sulla founded an Isiac college in Rome (about 80 B.C.) and worship of Isis continued in Italy until the fifth century.

Above: domestic altar in the House of Neptune, the sea god. The Romans worshiped the spirits of hearth and home (Vesta, Lares, Penates and Janus) in the belief that they would protect them. Left: Etruscan bronze statue of the god Mars. As father of Romulus, who founded Rome, he was particularly important to the Romans. God of spring when Roman interests were primarily agricultural, he became god of battle when their interests became mainly military.

Jupiter with Zeus, Juno with Hera, Minerva with Athena and so forth. Myths about them grew up, with Greek elements woven into Roman tradition.

The Romans also adopted a collection of cryptic Greek oracles, the famous Sibylline Books, which priests consulted to learn the will of the gods in the face of perplexity or impending disaster. In the first century B.C., the speculations of Greek philosophers added a conception of immortality to the traditional Roman ancestor cults, which developed out of veneration for the protective spirit of the founder of the family.

The formalism of state religion and Roman receptivity to the gods of conquered territories contributed to the unity of the Roman empire. To strengthen further the legitimacy of the empire, Roman emperors deified their predecessors, permitted worship of their protective spirits and later the emperors themselves were worshiped.

An alabaster statue of Artemis (or Diana) of Ephesus, one of the names under which the Egyptian goddess Isis came to be worshiped throughout the Roman Empire. The cult of Isis, which aimed at raising believers above the bestiality of their own natures and sharpening their spiritual perceptions, so ensuring eternal happiness, was particularly popular with women and rivaled Christianity.

Roman Mystery Cults

As in Greece, the religion of Rome lost its appeal for two groups of followers as it became increasingly formalized. The highly moralistic philosophy of the Greek Stoics (p. 96) attracted a large following among the educated Romans, who found in it an ethical pattern of behavior in an ordered universe. Mystery cults drew followers from those who needed the personal satisfaction of emotional worship. As the Roman Empire expanded throughout the Mediterranean region, soldiers, traders and colonists came to venerate the gods of the conquered areas.

One of the first cults to be transplanted to Rome was that of the Phrygian goddess Cybele (the *magna mater* or great mother). The Dionysian cult was introduced from Greece, and those of Ma of Cappadocia and Adonis of Syria followed. Some cults were banned by the Roman Senate. Others were officially supervised or sanctioned. Among them, two gods, Isis from Egypt and Mithras from Persia, received official recognition and became important throughout the empire. For a time they rivaled Christianity.

Unlike many other mother goddesses worshiped in Mediterranean cultures, the Egyptian Isis could also be regarded as a universal deity. Ptolemy I, the Macedonian king of Egypt (306–285 B.C.), had established a version of the Osiris cult in lower Egypt during the third century B.C. It then spread to the Hellenistic world and was recognized in Rome in the first century A.D. At first the ritual focused on Osiris, his wife-sister Isis, and their son Horus. Then Isis gradually became the most important of the three.

The Isis mysteries were particularly popular with women. The Romans regarded Isis as the savior of the living who could lead the initiate into light and sharpen spiritual perception. Illumination of the ritual could give followers a sense of participation in the divine nature and an assurance of immortal blessedness.

The cult of Mithras was distinctly masculine. Men of the Roman legions were attracted to it in Persia and carried it to Rome and other parts of the empire—as far as the border between England and Scotland. Mithras was a god of light, heat, fertility and generally the dispenser of the good things conducive to a healthy body and soul. As the eye of Ahura Mazda, he was the most powerful enemy of darkness and sin. Legends vary, but Mithras is nearly always associated with the bull. According to Persian mythology, the bull was the first creature ever made, and as such was a symbol of fertility. The various representations of Mithras mastering or slaying the bull emphasize his association with death and rebirth. As a god of light, Mithras ruled the lightning, symbolized by arrows or spears. The legionnaires worshiped him as a war god as well.

The rites of Mithraism involved a kind of baptism with the blood of a freshly-killed bull, which gave divine properties to the initiate. The celebrations included a sacramental meal of bread and wine to commemorate Mithras' partaking of the grain and vines which sprang up after the death of the sacred bull. One of the reasons Mithraism was slow in giving way to Christianity was this similarity in their rituals. Another was its immense popularity among the military (a key class), who worshiped Mithras as *sol invictus*, the unconquerable sun. Roman emperors adopted the cult in the second century. Any man could rise through its various grades and stages (there were no priests), so it had further influence as a bond of solidarity. However, Mithraism never was a faith with universal appeal, a factor that contributed to its eventual decline.

Above: Mithras, invincible sun god, slays a bull, symbolizing the victory of good over evil. At the *taurobolium* (latin for "bull-sacrifice") the initiate to the cult of Mithras was baptized in bull's blood. He could later share in a sacramental meal of bread and wine, symbols of Mithras' banquet after the sacrifice.

Below: wall painting of the rites of Bacchus from the Villa of the Mysteries in Pompeii (first century B.C.). The cult of Bacchus sprang from that of Dionysus, Greek god of wine, whose followers believed in ritual intoxication. In 186 B.C. the Senate tried to eliminate the orgiastic aspects of the cult, but without success.

GREAT RELIGIONS OF ASIA

Between the ninth and sixth centuries B.C., the world's major religious traditions assumed concrete form. In all there was a move away from polytheism. Hinduism, Buddhism, Confucianism and Taoism were based on a belief in an underlying, impersonal Reality, which either transcended or repudiated the cults of many gods. Further west, Zoroastrianism developed a kind of monotheism; and in Judaism, which later formed the basis of Christianity and Islam, monotheism emerged fully.

A Burmese girl celebrates the Enlightenment of the Buddha. The major religions of the world—Taoism, Confucianism, Hinduism and Buddhism in the East, and Zoroastrianism and Judaism, basis of Islam and Christianity, in the West—crystallized into their set forms between 800 and 500 B.C.

Early Hinduism

Some aspects of Hinduism existed before it assumed its name from the Persian word for India, Hind. Its complexity of terms and doctrines has encompassed a great range of religious belief and practice. Hindus can be atheists, pantheists, polytheists or agnostics within the framework of beliefs and institutions which maintains a doctrine of reincarnation: By properly observing the ethics of one system of behavior or another, a Hindu can improve his spirit and be reborn into a superior caste or even as a higher form of being.

The variety of Hindu belief and practice probably derives in part from doctrines of the advanced Bronze Age civilization on the Indus River. Some scholars have speculated that their religion provided the seeds of the Hindu doctrines of transmigration of souls and *karma* (fate, or destiny).

The Indo-European (or Aryan) tribes who swept through the Indus Valley 4,000 years ago imposed their customs and traditions on the people they conquered. The chieftain (or *rajah*) of each tribe surrounded himself with priests, whose job was to secure divine blessings for the chieftain and his people. Originally, the father of each family served as family priest. Their religion began with gods representing various aspects of nature, magic spells, sacrifices, myths and folk tales.

By the eighth century B.C., many of the hymns and prayers to ancient nature gods were written down in the *Rig-Veda*. (*Rig* means verses of praise, and *Veda*, related to the words wit and wisdom, means knowledge.) Its writings reveal a movement toward fusion of the various gods into a related cosmic unity. It contained appeals to Dyaus Pitar, the sky father; Prithivi Mater, the earth mother; Indra, the storm god; and Varuna, guardian of *rta*, the principle of cosmic order. Interspersed were hymns of special interest to the priests who performed the sacrifices: to Soma, god of the intoxicating ceremonial juice offered as a libation; Agni, god of the fire which made sacrifices effective; and to Brahmanaspati, the divine power of the sacred words of prayer. There were no temples or sacred areas, but altars were put up outdoors on special occasions. Soma, milk, food and animals were offered to the gods in elaborate ceremonies.

One hymn near the end of the *Rig-Veda* expresses the astonishingly advanced philosophical tendencies of at least some of the priests. It is a series of questions about the One Thing—the creator of the universe. "The gods came later than the earth's creation. Who knows then out of what the world has issued? Whether he (the Sole One, the One Thing) made the world or did not make it, he knows where this creation comes from... but then perhaps he knows not!"

By the time the invaders had begun to settle down, four distinct social classes were emerging: warriors, priests (Brahmans), ordinary people and the more or less enslaved original population. The Brahmans regarded themselves as the pivotal agencies of the universe. Their elaborate and often month-long rituals became more significant than the gods themselves. The *Brahmanas*, prose works added to the earlier Vedic writings, exhaustively detail the practices of different religious schools.

A third body of Hindu religious literature, the *Upanishads* ("sittings near a teacher"), relates the profound questioning of the period before 300 B.C. They are largely dialogues between teachers and pupils, and some scholars believe that nobles as well as Brahmans composed them. Men and women of all classes attempt to learn what reality is, and how much of the universe is merely appearance. All that is objective is Brahma, the Supreme Being. Some sections of the *Upanishads* state that the *atman*, or soul, is also Brahma. The nature of reality—a tree, the universe, a soul—is expressed in the phrase "Tat tvam asi" (You are it). Oneness with Brahma, the highest existence, can be achieved through many reincarnations only by strict respect for the law of karma, according to which everything a man does affects his ultimate destiny. A good man of low caste can be reborn as a noble or a bad man as a worm in the inexorable and impersonal cycle of existence in reincarnations.

Above: a Brahman, member of the priestly caste that established itself in later Vedic times. The elaborate, lengthy rituals described in the *Brahmanas* (sacred Hindu writings) were instigated by them and became even more important than the gods themselves.

Above: a swami, or holy hermit, in front of his cave. The Hindu religion embraces a wide variety of religious beliefs, maintaining that there are many paths to attaining "oneness with Brahma."

Above: bas-relief of Vishnu, the preserver, who, with Shiva the destroyer and Brahma the creator, formed the Hindu "Trinity." The god of cosmic order and goodness, Vishnu was worshiped with devotion rather than fear. Hindus think of the Buddha as one of the reincarnations of Vishnu.

Right: wood carving from South India of Agni, the Vedic god of fire, who was later worshiped as the purifier of sacrificial offerings. He is seen holding a torch and sacrificial spoon which are connected with the elaborate rituals of the Brahmans; he wears their cord of caste around his neck.

Left: Shiva, the destroyer, seated with Parvati, his powerful consort, who was a personification of female beauty (19th-century Hindu sculpture). The other gods urged their marriage, finally arranged by Kama, god of love, as it would produce Karttikeya, god of war.

Left: Hindu pilgrims bathe in the Ganges, the sacred river which they believe will wash away sin. The Hindu can obtain special blessings by making pilgrimages to holy places. Every year about 250,000 pilgrims go to Allahabad, where the Ganges and Jumna rivers meet, to join in the Magh-mela festival held there during the Hindu month of Magh.

Hinduism: Later Developments

The basic pessimism of Hinduism, that it is nearly impossible to live so perfectly that the spirit will obtain final release from the inexorable "wheel" of reincarnation and fuse with Brahma, led to a variety of attempts to find release from the cumulative miseries of existence. The nobles resented the social and religious implications of Brahmanism and the power and pretensions of its priests. The Brahmans, by absorbing rival variations of their religion instead of attacking their adherents as heretics, prevailed. They astutely tolerated cults of other deities and accepted elements of Jainism and Buddhism (p. 30), which began as reactions to Brahmanist orthodoxy.

Philosophically, three paths to salvation were recognized. The way of works emphasized systematic and methodical performance of traditional rites, with sharply defined legalistic social duties which enhanced a man's karma. The way of knowledge also included strict observance of caste rules and religious ceremonies, and a dedication to asceticism (to escape the sensual pleasure and pain which obscure reality). After studying the religious writings, and marrying and having children, the seeker after knowledge was to abandon all attachments to the world and become a hermit. Through meditation as a holy man, he would seek total knowledge of union with the universe. These two ways appealed largely to the rich and well-educated Brahmans and nobles.

Most common people followed the way of devotion, which encouraged love of a particular god, worship and surrender to him. The great literary monument, the *Bhagavad-Gita* (Song of the Blessed Lord) has had a profound influence on Hinduism since it was written over 1,000 years ago. Its warrior hero turns to the god Krishna, who advises: "Let right deeds be your motive, not the fruit which comes from them." Krishna is a kindly incarnation of the awesome god Vishnu, Supreme Lord and god of preservation.

Left: the non-Aryan Hindu goddess, Kali the Black, was venerated as a killer of demons. The wife of Shiva, she was once associated with ritual animal sacrifices, a practice no longer observed.

Whether they choose the way of works, the way of knowledge or the way of devotion, Hindus tolerate and respect each of the paths to release. They share a common belief in the pervasiveness of indescribable Brahma and the continuity of man's *atman*. The entire spectrum of beliefs and practices which Hinduism has absorbed are reflected in the otherwise apparently inconsistent customs and institutions which have developed from and around it. For a Hindu there is nothing inconsistent in praying to a different deity for different things. He can worship anywhere—alone on the road, for example—or lead family domestic rites, or watch priests conducting a ceremony at a local temple. He can also obtain special blessings by participating in religious festivals or by going on pilgrimages to holy places. There are hundreds of holy places, from local streams to famous ancient temples. To wash sin away in the Ganges, said to flow from Vishnu's feet in heaven, is holiest of all.

If, as ascetic forms of Hinduism preach, all life is sacred, some forms of reincarnation rank higher than others. Brahmans are highly respected. Although members of the Brahman caste are no longer always priests (and although modern India is attempting to destroy the undemocratic caste system), they are generally expected to have superior sanctity. The most highly respected of all are gurus, or religious teachers, and the holy men (yogis, sannyasis and sadhus) who mortify the flesh in order to liberate the spirit.

One reaction to early Hinduism presents an extreme form of asceticism. The fifth vow of Jainist monks sums up its basic tenets: "I renounce all attachments, whether to little or much, small or great, living or lifeless things." Its belief in the sanctity of all life greatly influenced medieval Hinduism, and Jainism continues to have a number of adherents around Bombay. Since it forbids taking life of any kind, Jains cannot practice a number of occupations; but many have prospered and earned social respect as lawyers, bankers and businessmen.

Left: Kandariya Mohadeo at Khajuraho, Central India, is a typical Hindu temple. Built about A.D. 1000, it is a model of the world constructed in the shape of a mountain. Right: busy street in Chandri Chowk in old Delhi, India. Traffic has to avoid sacred cows ambling in the road and sitting on the pavements.

Buddhism

Like Jainism (p. 29), Buddhism began as a reaction to Brahmanist Hinduism, but it rejects the way of asceticism for a "middle path." Its founder appears to have been a historical person, Siddhartha Gautama (about 566–480 B.C.), who was born in the foothills of the Himalayas, the son of a local chieftain. According to legend, he was protected from all unpleasantness and brought up in great luxury. He married a perfect woman, and after the birth of a son, set out on holy wanderings, shaving his head and putting on the coarse yellow robes of a religious mendicant.

Gautama was one of a great body of holy Brahman wanderers, and he studied Brahmanism with first one ascetic guru, then another. He practiced the rigid deprivations and mortifications of extreme Jainism—never washing, exposing his body to the elements, starving himself almost to death. In six years of searching, Gautama failed to find satisfaction until he wandered to a place called Buddh Gaya and sat down under a tree to meditate. Under this tree (later called the Knowledge, or Bo, tree), he underwent profound religious ecstasy and found clarity: Desire or craving is the reason for human unhappiness; absence of desire the way to salvation. From this experience Siddhartha Gautama became Buddha, the Enlightened One. In the deer park at Benares he preached his first sermon to five ascetics who no longer respected him. In the course of several days, he converted them to the "middle way" between self-indulgence and mortification.

As he wandered over northern India, Buddha rapidly gathered disciples from all castes. The tenets of Buddhism were codified; and a monastic order, the Sangha, was formed. After 45 years of teaching, Buddha died near where he was born, after an attack of what may have been food poisoning.

Buddha's philosophy was concerned more with feelings than with strict philosophy. He rejected the way of devotion to the gods as well as the ascetic extremes. He reinterpreted the law of karma humanistically. A man who freed himself from human desire and its attendant miseries achieved *nirvana*. He was liberated from the ceaseless wheel of reincarnation. Buddha's doctrine of rebirth was rather more baffling. Summed up as "There is no ego here to be found," no substantive soul passing from one

Top: a massive statue of Buddha reclining, in the Shwehmawdaw Pagoda in Pegu, Burma. Below: the Golden Bull at one entrance to the Temple of the Emerald Buddha. The gold leaf on its nose is the offering of worshipers.

Left: the sixth century stupa at Buddh Gaya, which is the most sacred shrine in the Buddhist world. It marks the site of the tree (later known as the Knowledge, or Bo, tree) under which Buddha sat down to meditate and first achieved enlightenment.

form to another in the round of reincarnation, he compared the process of rebirth to one flaming torch lighting another. The fire is transferred without any measurable amount of flame being lost. As longing and desire are so constantly characteristic of human beings, they clearly are transferred in each rebirth. If they could be annihilated the chief cause of rebirth would be no more.

Buddha's ethical teachings were designed to obliterate human craving in all aspects of life (except those which decrease the sum total of misery in the world) and particularly to remove spiritual ignorance. Their basic formulation is the Noble Eightfold Path, which leads to absence of desire: (1) Right belief: abandon the desires that bring any misery to anyone at all, encourage desires which bring relief from misery; (2) Right purpose: overcome the temptations of the senses, harm no living being and love all living beings; (3) Right speech; (4) Right conduct; (5) Right means of livelihood; (6) Right effort; (7) Right mindfulness; (8) Right meditation: to know the truth after the other seven precepts have cleared the mind for it.

Above: the elaborately decorated and ornamented interior of the temple of Wat Po in Bangkok, Siam. A saffron-robed *bonze* (Buddhist monk) sits in prayer before the golden statue of the Buddha. Below: an image of the Buddha in the White Marble Temple in Bangkok. As above, the statue is sitting in the "lotus posture," a position common to many forms of Asian meditation.

The Vehicles of Salvation

Above: Bodhnath Temple, Nepal (273–232 B.C.). Its structure reflects the Buddhist world-view. The stepped pyramid on top represents the thirteen heavens of the gods; the dome symbolizes the sky and the all-seeing eyes of Buddha look out between them. Right: Buddhist monks stage a demonstration before the elections in South Vietnam to demand a non-military government. Buddhism is still a powerful and vocal force in that country.

By 200 B.C., Buddhism had begun to spread throughout Asia and had developed two distinct forms: the Greater and Lesser Vehicles of salvation. The Lesser Vehicle, or Hinayana, was originally an abusive title resulting from the emphasis on salvation rather than concern for others. Predominant in Ceylon, Cambodia and Thailand, it is close to the original teachings of Buddha. For its followers the goal of nirvana means the destruction of individuality. Great emphasis is placed on solitary contemplation in monasteries. In Thailand and Burma, it is common for most young men to spend several months in a monastery, studying and meditating.

The Lesser Vehicle regards Buddha as having a divine nature, but not as a god in the sense of other religions. There were other Buddhas before him, and another may come again to teach men the true way. Temples are full of images of Buddha and his disciples, and offerings from the faithful. Although ordinary people may believe that Buddha is a divine personality who can hear and answer their prayers, the learned monks regard prayer as something which increases merit, but not as part of a dialogue.

What characterizes the Greater Vehicle, or Mahayana, is its religious appeal. In its oldest form there was nothing really religious about Buddhism. There were no gods, no prayers, no sacrifices, no meaningful worship and no concept of a meaningful world. Kindly concern for living creatures and a preoccupation with losing oneself through meditation provide a noble way for the philosophical to try to reach salvation, but lack sufficient guidance and personal comfort for most ordinary people.

Mahayana recognizes three kinds of Buddhas. The groups contain Buddhas whose concerns are often specific functions or needs—sometimes identified with earlier local nature deities. Bodhisattvas are like Gautama before his enlightenment. Manushi Buddhas, like Buddha, have been enlightened teachers on earth. They have achieved nirvana and prayers can no longer reach them. Dhyani Buddhas never come to earth, but wait in heaven ministering to men's needs until they attain nirvana.

As most ordinary people's lives do not enable them to achieve nirvana through meditation, they can turn to the Bodhisattvas, who postpone enlightenment and nirvana in order to help others achieve salvation. Mahayana holds that everyone is a potential Buddha, although it may take many incarnations. Unlike Hinayana, which recognizes neither gods nor an absolute, Mahayana more optimistically identifies nirvana with an underlying absolute; and release from reincaranation becomes union with the absolute rather than nothing.

Mahayana spread to China in the first century A.D. and reached Japan about A.D. 500. Devotional, rational and intuitive sects developed in China, and "true word" political and Zen (a form of intuition) sects in Japan. In both places the filial piety encouraged in Buddhism could be incorporated in their traditional ancestor worship.

In Tibet, Nepal and Mongolia, Buddhism took a different form, sometimes called Third Vehicle. It absorbed elements of local demonology and a form of Hinduism called tantraism, which holds that desires are destroyed by first satisfying and then rising above them. Tantraism also says that the human body is the universe in microscosm and is as susceptible to spells and incantations as the elements and deities.

The three practices which have traditionally characterized Tibetan Buddhism are the importance it accords to religious formulas to ward off evil spirits and remind the gods that believers' hearts are in the right place; the large number of believers who become monks or nuns; and their unusual method of choosing a spiritual leader, or Lama. The practice involves finding a child born at the moment the old Lama died and offering him relics of the old Lama to express his religious vocation.

Top: a Tibetan worshiper stands at the entrance of a Buddhist shrine. In Tibet Buddhism combined with the indigenous religion. Above: a statue of the Buddha (17th century A.D.) in Nara, Japan. Here Mahayana, a mystical and emotional form of Buddhism, prevails.

Confucius and Lao-tzu

Above: 17th-century painting of Confucius who lived in the sixth century B.C. and taught that the Golden Age lay in the past. His five books of "Li" (correct behavior) were intended to teach men the path to goodness in an inferior age so that a just Chinese society be reestablished. (Courtesy Museum of Fine Arts, Boston. Fenollosa-Weld Collection.)

Left: Lao-tzu riding a water buffalo (Taoist painting). The originator of Taoism, Lao-tzu believed the harmony of the universe should be maintained by complete passivity, men should accept their fate, not attempting to improve themselves. This attitude led to a contemplative way of life.

When Mahayana Buddhism began to spread through China in the first century A.D., the Chinese already possessed an ancient cosmology full of spirits and demons rather than gods, a cult of fertility, ancestor-worship and a great body of myths.

Their apparently inconsistent beliefs had been further influenced by the philosophical teachings of two men, roughly contemporary with Buddha. K'ung Fu-tzu, or Confucius (551–478 B.C.), lived during a period of political upheaval and military strife. China was composed of many independent states, feudalism prevailed, and there was no commonly-accepted religion. Accepting China's ancestor-worship, Confucius taught that utopia, or the Golden Age, lay in the past, and that men were lapsing from their native goodness and the natural harmony of the universe.

The secret of achieving natural harmony, personally and collectively, lay in the principle of *Li*—an untranslatable word for good behavior, what one is, how things should be. Adherence to external patterns and forms would produce internal grace or brightness. *Li* meant a rigid stratification of status and duties to eliminate the misery of anarchy. Fathers and kings should be shown the respect due to fathers and kings, who in turn were supposed to treat their sons and subjects with wisdom and benevolence. This reciprocity was allied to an ethic of "deal with people as if you were assisting at a great sacrifice, and do not do to them what you would not wish to be done to yourself."

Confucius compiled five books to expound the *Li* of the Golden Age. Studying a better past and following its rites and forms could teach a man to be good in his inferior age. The dangers of the benevolent ethics of Confucianism are clear: fossilization and empty formalism, and later rigid conservatism and legalism.

Lao-tzu, who may or may not have been a historical person, is said to have lived and taught just before Confucius (about 604–517 B.C.). His importance lies in his association with the other great influence on Chinese beliefs and behavior—Taoism. Like Confucianism, Taoism teaches that harmony results from permitting the universe, and the people and things in it, to take their natural

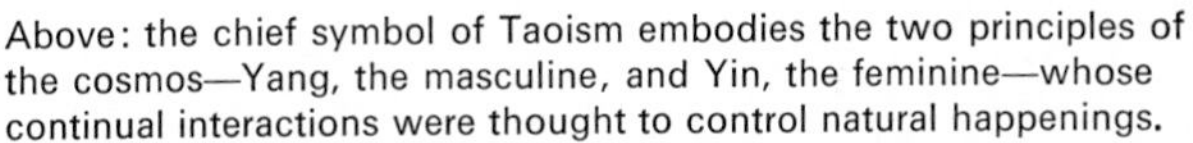

Above: the chief symbol of Taoism embodies the two principles of the cosmos—Yang, the masculine, and Yin, the feminine—whose continual interactions were thought to control natural happenings.

Left: plan of the temple of Hua Yin Hsien in the province of Shensi. For centuries Chinese emperors sacrificed to the mountain on which it stands, a social duty of the ruler appointed by heaven.

course. But its great book, the *Tao Te Ching* (A Treatise on the Tao and its Virtue) makes it clear how different is its view of the world. Tao means the way, path or channel—the underlying reality of all things, which ought never to be disturbed. Men are neither all good nor all bad, nor should they seek to improve themselves: "The swan does not need a daily washing to stay white; the crow does not need a daily inking to stay black." Men's natures cannot be changed.

The chief symbol of Taoism shows the two principles of the cosmos, Yang and Yin, in constant interaction and flux. Yang is masculine, heaven, positive, strong, active, sun, light and odd. Yin is feminine, earth, negative, weak, passive, moon, dark and even. Man must conform to the interplay of Yang and Yin, and not try to change the Tao of anything in the universe. The doctrine of inactivity explicit in Taoism encourages contemplation and passivity—acceptance of life rather than ambition to change it—for "The Tao is always inactive, yet there is nothing that it does not do."

Popular Taoism became inextricably mixed up with ancient Chinese demonology and magic, traditional alchemy and medicine, and even art. The connection may be rooted in a search for the Tao of everything and its power. A Chinese nature painting is not a naturalistic reproduction of a particular mountain or tree, but an attempt to capture the essence, or Tao, of the tree or mountain.

The extension of Buddhism's emphasis on contemplation and nonviolence did not entirely compete with China's ancient demons and ancestors or the ethics of Confucius and spiritual passivity of Taoism. The interplay of all these produced China's strong family ties and ability to bend with the Tao of what happens and not break.

Contemplation forms an important part of all the principal Eastern religions.
Below: an Indian holy man rests outside his cave home. In the foothills of the Himalayas holy sages, yogis, sannyasis and sadhus, all hermits of differing shades of religious belief, live a life of solitary contemplation. Buddhists and Hindus have developed techniques of meditation which, by divorcing the mind from the physical limitations of the body, bring divine illumination and understanding. The Buddhist believes this can be done by fixing the mind on a simple object such as a flower, clearing the mind of all else and, finally, obliterating the object itself, leaving the mind free of earthly thoughts and ready to receive spiritual insight. Zen Buddhism stresses the spontaneity of such illumination, but this must be prefaced by years of dedictated training and preparation.
Left: the calligraphy of the monk Ryokwan (1758–1831) is a superb example of the simplicity of Zen art, which, like meditation, must transcend the necessary elaborate training.
Below left: a Zen Buddhist monk rakes the sand in a Japanese monastery garden. The arrangement of stones and sand is such as to provide an object of contemplation for the adept. As in the contemplation of works of art, the believer may perceive truth and beauty and gain enlightenment. Hindus who practice the doctrine of Yoga concentrate more on the physical methods by which a state of complete tranquillity can be achieved.
Right: a Fakir from Benares, his tongue pierced by two pieces of wood and his begging bowl at his side, is sitting in one of the traditional Yoga postures. More advanced postures include difficult balancing and breathing exercises that can only be achieved by the greatest concentration and years of practice. By freeing the soul from its earthly nature the Hindu can escape from the cycle of death, rebirth and suffering. Recently, there has been a new interest in meditation in the Western world.
Bottom: Maharishi Mahesh Yogi with the Beatles and film star Mia Farrow when they went to study at the academy of Transcendental Meditation in India. The interest of such a famous pop group has drawn much attention to this form of meditation.

Zoroastrianism

Above: winged symbol of Ahura Mazda, from Persepolis (about 500 B.C.). Zoroaster preached a dualistic religion in which Ahura Mazda, the "Wise Lord," was the only god. The existence of evil was believed to be due to independent spirits who were at war with him. Below: Roman statue of Ahriman, the supreme hostile spirit, who is depicted here as a lion-headed god. Ahriman later appeared in the Roman cult of Mithras as the evil "prince of this world."

Today there are only a small number of Zoroastrians, most of whom live in Iran and India, chiefly in Bombay where they are known as Parsees (Persians). The religion they practice is a dualistic form of an ethical monotheism which arose in what is now Iran. Zoroastrianism developed after Judaism and independently of it.

Zoroaster (or Zarathustra), like Moses and Mohammed, was a prophet whose visions led him to call his people back to a purer faith. Pre-Zoroastrian Persian religion was a polytheism closely related to that of Indo-Europeans in Vedic India (p. 25). The legends about Zoroaster give him a miraculous conception and later persecution. It seems likely that he was the son of a pastoral chieftain, born about 600 B.C. After an apparently blameless life at home, he set out at 20 to follow the path of a religious wanderer. He questioned sages and, according to one myth, spent seven or more years in the wilderness before receiving a revelation at the age of 30. In Zoroaster's vision an angel, Vohu Manah (Good Thought), led him to the supreme being, Ahura Mazda (the Wise Lord). Following Ahura Mazda's instructions, Zoroaster preached, unsuccessfully at first, a doctrine of monotheism: one god and the moral behavior he required.

His attempt to grapple with the problem of evil in the world continues to puzzle scholars. Apparently, although both good and evil spirits flourished in the world, Ahura Mazda was the only god, expressing his will through various modes of good: Benevolent Thoughts, Right, Power, Prosperity, Piety, and so on. (In early Persian religion Ahura Mazda himself was an important god concerned with morals and ethics.) Opposed to them are evil spirits including Druj, the Lie, and Angra Mainyu, the Bad Spirit, who later was called Ahriman.

Eschatology—the conception of final things—appears in Zoroastrianism for the first time in world religion. At the end of each world age comes a general resurrection, when men are judged by an ordeal of fire and molten metal and either punished or rewarded. Each individual will also be judged at the end of his own life. A sunny paradise full of companions awaits virtuous men, and isolation in darkness awaits the unrighteous.

Zoroaster preached a final and perfect religion and taught that the seat of the war between good and evil is in man. Man is given the freedom to choose by Ahura Mazda. Zoroaster attacked the traditional polytheistic worship, and the magic and idolatry of the old Indo-European rites.

After two years of failure, Zoroaster converted King Vishtaspa; and the new faith flourished and spread. As it developed it changed, as occasionally conflicting information in different parts of its holy book, the *Zend Avesta*, reveals. Although Ahura Mazda (or Ormazd as he was later called) remained supreme, Zoroaster came to be worshiped for miraculous powers, and some of the old gods crept back in, especially Mithras as a god of light and war. Fire became an important symbol in Zoroastrian ritual.

Holy wars extended Zoroastrianism and the Magi, a mysterious and influential group of Medeans (whose skills give us the word magic), supported it. The great kings of the Persian Empire, Cyrus (about 558–529 B.C.), Darius (521–486 B.C.) and Xerxes (about 486–465 B.C.), honored Ahura Mazda. It is possible that only the defeat of Xerxes at Salamis, when he was attempting to invade Greece in 480 B.C., checked Zoroastrianism's growth as a major world religion. Within a century of the Moslem conquest of Persia in the seventh century A.D., it had become the religion of emigrants to India and a few faithful in Persia.

Above: a figure probably representing Zoroaster from the Mithraeum at Dura-Europos, now set up at Yale University, Yale University Art Gallery. Said to be the son of a pastoral chief, Zoroaster was born about 600 B.C. He attacked the traditional polytheistic worship of his native Persia and preached a doctrine of monotheism.

Right: the decapitated body of the Persian Mani (A.D. 216–77), whose execution was instigated by the priests of Zoroaster (painting from a 14th-century Islamic manuscript). Mani was the founder of Manicheanism, a faith that incorporated aspects of Zoroastrianism, Buddhism and Christianity.

Ancient Judaism

The Hebrews worshiped a god long before his name, Yahweh, was revealed to Moses during their Egyptian bondage. Abraham, who is believed to have migrated to the land of the Philistines (Palestine) about 1800 B.C., had a personal experience of a supreme God so powerful that he obeyed him utterly. The generations of Hebrews following him recognized this God as well. Invasion or famines (as in the story of Joseph) forced them to migrate to the borders of Egypt. At some point they were compelled to offer forced labor for a pharaoh's public works, and were kept in bondage until Moses released them and led them back to Canaan.

The great achievement of Moses was not the recognition of Yahweh, but the revelation of his omnipotence. He reminded the Hebrews that their God was different, superior to the *baalim*, the local nature spirits of other neighboring peoples. Moses served as the intermediary between God and the Hebrews in their covenant—the unique essence of Judaism. The God who sent Moses to lead them from Egypt chose the Hebrews to serve him, and they chose him. The Ten Commandments handed down on Mount Sinai—which have had more influence than any other single code in history—formed the core of their side of the bargain. Old Testament history is an interpretation of how well they kept it.

By about 1200 B.C., the conquest of Palestine had turned the nomadic Hebrews into a settled, agricultural people. They sacrificed to Yahweh in seasonal ceremonies like those of neighboring peoples. Their religious leaders were continually alert to the possibility of people reverting to worship of local baalim. It seemed a question of whether the faith would assimilate the strong appeal of the baalim, or whether worship of Yahweh would be diffused among them. In the struggle for supremacy, Judaism was interpreted by inspired men, not usually priests, who called its people back from idolatry to the austere worship of Yahweh. These were the Prophets.

The prosperity of the age of Solomon (10th century B.C.), whose magnificent temple became the center of Jewish worship, was followed by a division of the kingdom. In the eighth century B.C., the Assyrians destroyed the northern kingdom of Israel; and its ten tribes scattered to surrounding nations. Two centuries later, Jerusalem, in the southern kingdom of Judah, fell to the Babylonians, who took the Jews to Babylonia as captives.

In this period, faith was kept alive by the Prophets who told the Jews that their defeat and exile were a result of disobedience and disloyalty to Yahweh.

Above: Moses descends from Mount Sinai holding the tablets of stone inscribed with the Ten Commandments given to him by God for the guidance and salvation of the Hebrew tribes he had led out of Egypt to freedom. (Illumination from the Sarajevo Haggadah, an ornamental Passover liturgy, executed in Spain in the 14th century.) Below: imaginary plan of Jericho enclosed within its seven legendary walls, an illustration from the 14th-century Fahri Bible. Jericho was captured by Joshua, Moses' successor, who led the Israelites out of the wilderness and into the land of Canaan.

Amos stressed the inevitability of Jehovah's punishments, the vanity of ceremonial sacrifice and the importance of righteousness—for God says: "I hate, I despise your feast days, but let judgment (justice) run down as waters and righteousness as a mighty stream." Hosea reminded his people that the harsh God who punished wrongdoing would reward the righteous with mercy and love. Isaiah preached a golden age of deliverance for the faithful after a day of doom for the evil. Jeremiah, in the critical period of the conquest of Jerusalem, wrote of a new, personal covenant between Jehovah and the individual: "I shall write my law in their hearts... and they shall all know me."

During the Babylonian Exile, which lasted until the Persian conquest in 538 B.C., when King Cyrus permitted the Jews to return to Jerusalem, certain aspects of Judaism altered. Not only did the concept of an individual covenant with God evolve, but the Jews came to believe that Yahweh was not just God of Israel but of all mankind. Judaism thus evolved from a *monolatrous* faith (one which worships its own single god but recognizes that other gods exist) to a universal monotheism. History was therefore the working out of God's purpose and as such had a unity and meaning lacking in other ancient religions. The Jews would be God's chosen people to bring salvation to the Gentiles (non-Jews).

Above: Abraham prepares to sacrifice his son Isaac in an act of supreme obedience to his God. (Detail from the sixth-century mosaic pavement of the Beth-Alpha synagogue in Israel.)
Below: wall-painting (from a synagogue in Mesopotamia of the third century A.D.) of Solomon's magnificent temple at Jerusalem, which became the center of Jewish worship in the 10th century B.C.

Judaism to the Time of Christ

Above: ravens bring food to Elijah at the brook of Cherith (12th-century French miniature) where he hid from the wrath of King Ahab (Bodleian MS. Bodley 270b, f.168).

During the period between the end of the Babylonian Exile and the time of Christ, Judaism was subject to a variety of external and internal influences. In the fourth century, the conquests of Alexander the Great (336–323 B.C.) led to a century and a half of Hellenistic rule and the extension of Hellenistic culture to Palestine. Because it was initially tolerant, the culture was an attractive influence; but when, in 168 B.C., a Hellenistic Syrian king sought to force the Jews to worship Zeus and Dionysus, they revolted under Judas Maccabaeus (died 160 B.C.). In 141 B.C. they founded an independent Jewish state. It lasted until 63 B.C. when the Roman general Pompey (106–48 B.C.), called in to arbitrate a dispute, took it over for Rome.

In addition to Hellenism—which emphasized wisdom, reason and common sense—Zoroastrianism (p. 38), with its evil spirits, angels and conception of a last judgment, influenced Judaism in this period. Various sects and factions developed among the faithful.

The Pharisees, a party which arose from the Hasidim (pious ones or puritans) who had supported Judas Maccabaeus, held that the Law was most important—not merely the basic Old Testament writings, but also the unwritten commentaries on the extensions of this law. Although they believed in the resurrection of the dead and the Last Judgment, they were hostile to Greco-Roman influences and other interpretations of their faith.

Opposing the Pharisees was the priestly faction, the Sadducees. They were more conservative about

Above: relief of the prophet Isaiah, who lived in the eighth century B.C., from the church of Souillac in southwest France (about A.D. 1140). When the Assyrian kings were molding the world by brute force, Isaiah prophesied the coming of the Messiah and the rise of a new Jerusalem where peace and righteousness would reign.

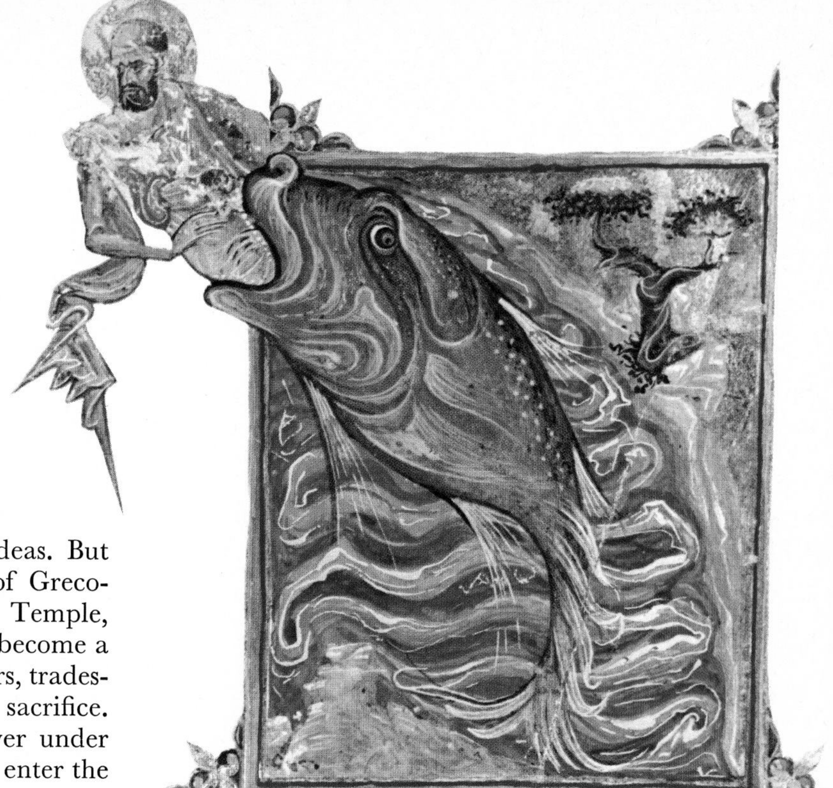

the Law, rejecting the new messianic ideas. But they were liberal in their acceptance of Greco-Roman culture. They controlled the Temple, which, rebuilt at the time of Christ, had become a huge complex of buildings housing teachers, tradesmen, moneychangers and animals for sacrifice. Although the Sadducees held their power under Roman authority, only Jews were able to enter the most sacred part of the Temple.

The Temple remained the center for sacrifice and ceremony, but ordinary worship was conducted at home or in a simple synagogue (Greek for meeting place). Other Jewish factions defined themselves without reference to the Temple. The Zealots were ardently patriotic and believed that submission to Roman rule meant forsaking God. Their bloody and unsuccessful revolt was also supposed to hasten the coming of the Messiah. Under Roman rule, expectation of the Messiah had become a vital reality for many Jews. He would be God's divine instrument for a radical change in the world order, possibly a military leader. He would bring blessedness for the righteous, punishment for the unfaithful and a light to the Gentiles.

One party believed to be preparing themselves for his coming were the Essenes, who lived an austere, communistic life on the shores of the Dead Sea. The Dead Sea Scrolls, found in 1947, do not make it clear how soon they expected this "Teacher of Righteousness."

Before his death, Herod (37–4 B.C.) had begun a magnificent rebuilding of the Temple. The Zealots, referred to as robber bandits by the Romans, had risen against Rome in expectation of the Messiah. Powerful and factious priestly parties controlled the temples, sacrifices and teaching of the Rabbis, concerning themselves with definition of the Law and the value of Greek and Roman culture. Groups like the Essenes withdrew from active life in the community. Hebrew was dying out as a language of the common people, who spoke Aramaic.

Above: Jonah emerges from the mouth of the whale (13th-century Armenian miniature). Jonah had tried to escape the task God gave him—to denounce the wicked city of Nineveh—by going to sea, but was thrown overboard in a storm and swallowed by a whale. He repented of his disobedience and was restored by God to dry land.

Above: the prophet Amos (illustration from the 12th-century Park Abbey Bible), a herdsman by birth, who left his flock to prophesy the imminence of the Day of Judgment. He was the prophet of moral righteousness, concerned that men should observe God's laws rather than becoming preoccupied with the vanity of ceremonial sacrifices.

Judaism since Christ

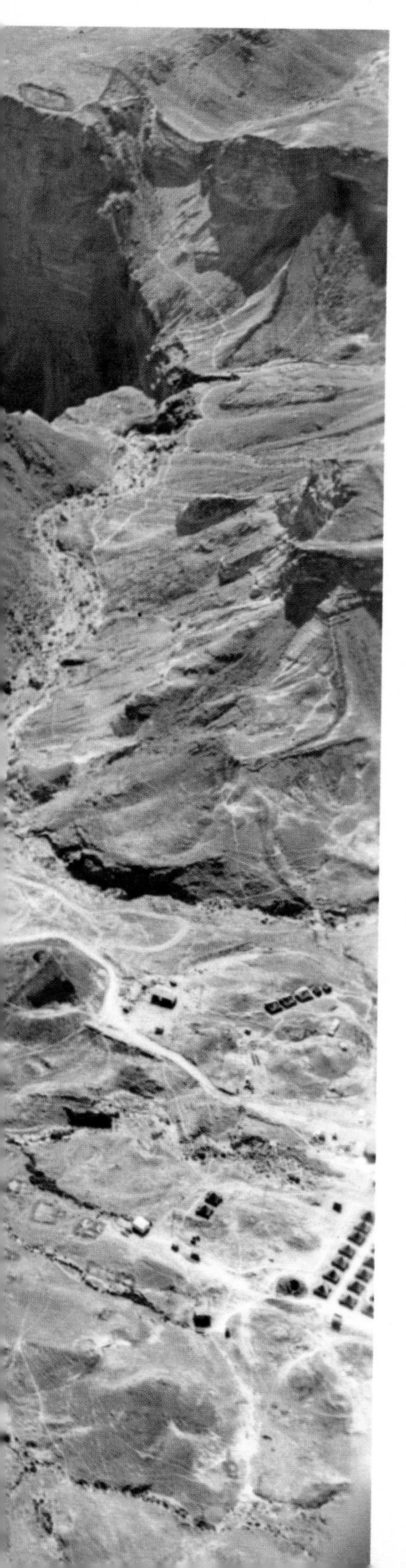

The history of Judaism since Jesus is one of a struggle for survival against successive persecutions. In A.D. 70, after a series of Jewish revolts, Titus, son of the Roman Emperor Vespasian, destroyed the Temple and razed the city of Jerusalem in an attempt to crush the Jews. Few Jewish rebels resisted after this. The last held the fortress of Massada, seen from the air (left). Recent excavations have revealed the Roman camp (bottom right of photo). The Jews holding the fortress on the plateau committed mass suicide when they saw their plight was hopeless. Sixty years later the Emperor Hadrian forbade Jews to enter Jerusalem except on one day in the year—the anniversary of the destruction of the Temple—when they were allowed to visit part of the old foundation wall, the Wailing Wall (below, as it is today). Driven out of their homeland and seeking freedom to worship, Jews spread into Turkey, then to Spain, where Jewish learning flourished under Moorish rule in the 10th and 11th centuries. They spread across western Europe in the Middle Ages, establishing new communities where they worshiped privately and quietly without the central focus of the Temple. But relations with the Christians, whom the Jews considered to be fanatical heretics, had been uneasy from the beginning and when the wave of enthusiasm for the Crusades swept Europe in the 11th century, anti-Jewish feeling among Christians rose high and the centuries of Jewish persecution began. Jews were officially expelled from England in the 13th century and driven from Spain and France in the 15th century. Up until the 18th century, Jews were confined to ghettos; they therefore developed their own ghetto mentality of protective isolation. Jewish prisoners are led through Warsaw in 1943 (above) after the ghetto there revolted against the German invaders. World War II saw the most vicious Jewish persecution of all time when Germany embarked on a brutal campaign to exterminate the whole race. Three years after the war Jews gained what the 19th-century Zionist movement had hoped for—a country of their own—when, in 1948, the state of Israel was created in the former Palestine. But Jerusalem was divided and part retained by the Arab state of Jordan. In the June war of 1967 the Israelis captured the Jordanian sector of Jerusalem and returned to worship at the Wailing Wall from which their forefathers had been expelled nearly two thousand years before.

CHRISTIANITY AND ISLAM

Christianity developed among Jews who were convinced that Jesus was the long-awaited Messiah. When Paul spread the Gospel to non-Jews, Christianity became a universal religion rather than one limited to people of Jewish birth. In the seventh-century Arab world, Islam, which derived partly from Judaism and Christianity, was proclaimed by the prophet Mohammed; and by the eighth century it had become a major religious force.

Jesus and his Ministry

Modern scholars generally agree that Jesus Christ was a historical person born in 4 B.C. (the discrepancy results from calculating errors when the Church decided, in the sixth century A.D., to reckon time from the birth of Christ) and put to death about 35 years later. They also agree that his life and teachings profoundly influenced many who knew him. The nature of information available about Jesus makes further certainty about him difficult. It consists largely of the four Gospels, which, with the rest of the New Testament, were written down only after his death.

Except for the story of the boy Jesus arguing theology with the elders in the Temple, very little is known about him until he was about 30. His family appears to have been religious. Mary's husband Joseph was a carpenter; and it is probable that when Joseph died, Jesus took over his work. When Jesus was about 30, John the Baptist left his solitary meditating in the wilderness to preach on the banks of the Jordan. His urgent message was that the coming of the Messiah was imminent.

John preached that God would save only those who genuinely repented of their sin and lived in strict righteousness. Immersion in water—baptism—was a visible symbol of repentance and the washing away of sin. Jesus heard John, was moved, and when he was baptized underwent a profound

Jesus delivers the Sermon on the Mount (by Beato Angelico in the Museum of S. Marco, Florence), which contained the core of his ethical teaching. His doctrine of humility and love toward all men did not appeal to many of the Jews who had expected the Messiah to be a powerful military leader.

Top left: painting of the Nativity from Bellieu Church in Bulgaria. Joseph and Mary kneel beside their son Jesus in the stable where he was born and the first shepherd comes to worship him. Left: the arrival of the three kings, who followed a brilliant star in the sky which led them to the infant Jesus. They presented him with gifts of gold, frankincense and myrrh befitting a king. Above: the Resurrection (from a 16th-century French missal). In spite of Roman guards, Jesus' body disappeared from the tomb. His disciples, their faith confirmed, believed he had risen from death.

religious experience: the spirit of God singling him out for his mission. He retired to the wilderness to meditate, where he faced and resisted three temptations concerning the course he was to take: material satisfaction, spectacular methods and political power.

For most of the next year (or three years) Jesus preached out of doors or in synagogues. He attracted vast crowds, including hecklers and questioners from the Pharisees and Sadducees, who feared the effect of his teaching. Although he did not openly claim to be the Messiah, the disciples closest to him were convinced that he was sent from God; and his teachings reinforced their conviction. He presented God as a merciful and loving father whose kingdom was almost at hand. All men are equal in his sight, and he loves them even when they sin. The God of Jesus is served by kindness and love rather than sacrifice, and he hears solitary prayer, not merely liturgical incantations.

Jesus' ethical teachings, summed up in the Sermon on the Mount, were full of the same religious assurance. As God loves everyone, those who in turn love him and their fellow beings will participate most fully in his kingdom. Affirming life, Jesus never viewed the human body or the reality of the human condition as corrupt, but his emphasis on a just spirit and the worth of the individual cast serious doubt on contemporary religious, political and social institutions, thereby attracting the hostility of both Roman and Jewish authorities.

The Romans, who had put down a Zealot uprising in A.D. 6, feared more rebellion from Messianic Jews. The Pharisees and Sadducees were offended by Jesus' disrespect for the Law and tradition, and others resented him for not being the military leader they expected as a Messiah. Against this background, identifying himself with the suffering servant prophesied by Isaiah, Jesus told his disciples that he had to go to Jerusalem to face

Above: Jesus raises Lazarus from the dead after he had been in his grave for four days (painting from the catacombs in Rome). This was one of the large number of miracles which Jesus performed during his ministry and which are recorded in the four Gospels. Top right: the Transfiguration. Jesus took the disciples Peter, James and John up a mountain; there they saw him in a different form—his face and figure transformed and shining—with Moses and Elijah at his side. Clearly the experience of intimacy with God did have a vivid effect on Jesus and, through him, on his disciples.

suffering and death for his mission to be fulfilled.

Thousands of Jews were in Jerusalem for the Passover festival; and the Roman governor, Pontius Pilate, was there to maintain order. The Jewish court, the Sanhedrin, charged Jesus with blasphemy for claiming to be the Messiah. Jesus was handed over to the Romans, who carried out the sentence of crucifixion. His body was taken from the cross so that it would not hang there on the Sabbath and put in an empty tomb by a member of the Sanhedrin, Joseph of Arimathaea. If Jesus' life had ended in the tomb, a local Jewish heretical sect might have died without a trace. Christianity begins with Christ's death, for on the third day after the crucifixion Mary Magdalene found the stone rolled away and the tomb empty. In the next 40 days the disciples were certain that he appeared again to them, that he rose from the dead and ascended into heaven, having charged them with a mission to spread his teachings throughout the world.

Above: the Last Supper before the betrayal of Jesus by Judas Iscariot (from the ninth-century rock church in Cappadocia). This scene is commemorated in the Eucharist—a basic Christian rite.

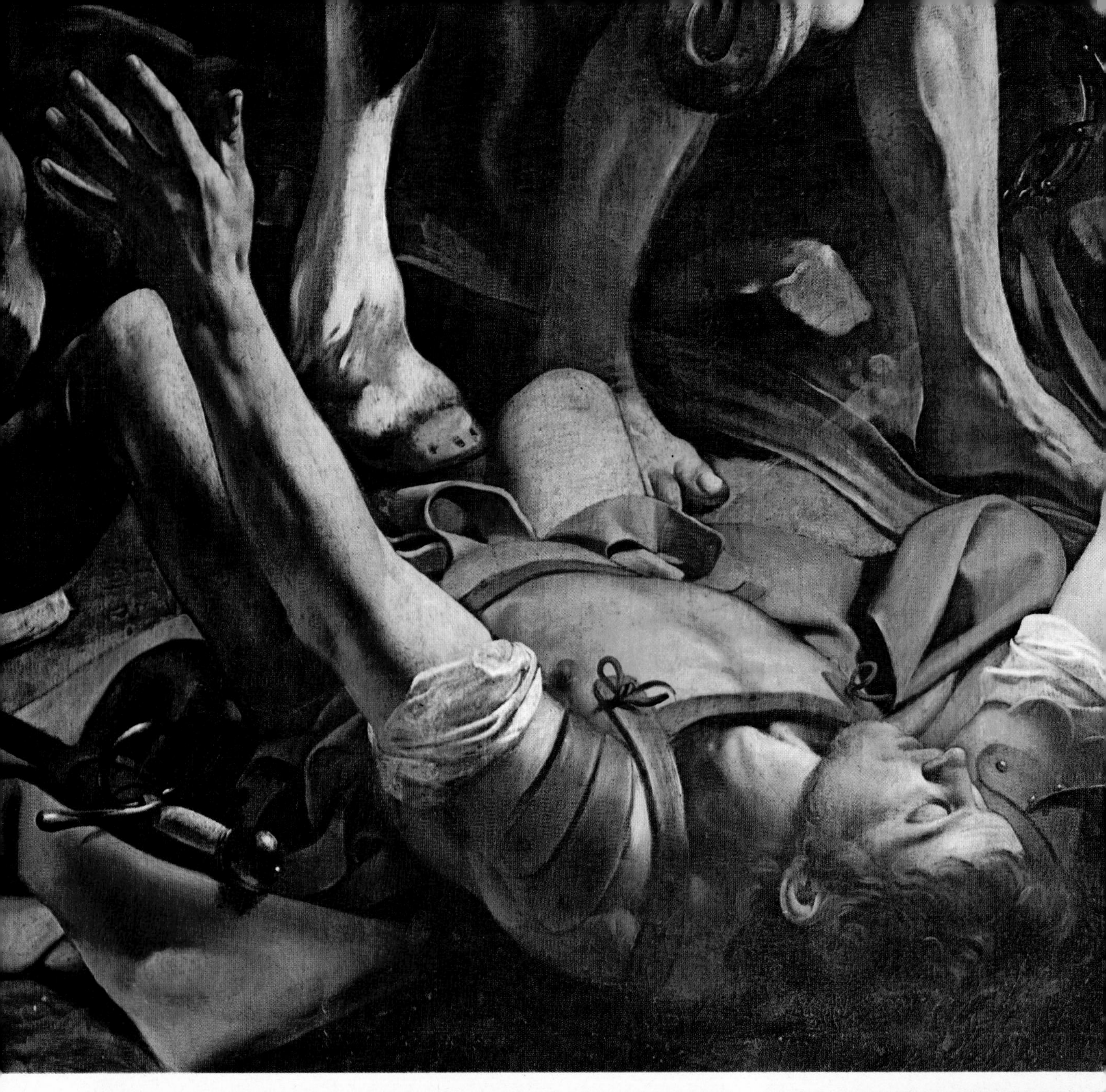

Paul and the Early Christians

The first Christians were divided into those who worshiped within the basic framework of orthodox Jewish laws and those converts whose cultural background was Hellenistic and who did not. The Jewish authorities in Jerusalem resented the Hellenistic or Greek sect and its compromises, and after putting to death Stephen, a liberal Christian, began to persecute all such heretics. One of the most zealous in the task of persecution was Saul, a Pharisee from Tarsus in southern Turkey. But on the way to Damascus to attack Christians there, he fell to the ground, blinded by a great light, and heard a voice crying "Saul, Saul, why do you persecute me?" The power of his vision is caught by Caravaggio's painting (left). Saul's entire life was altered. He was baptized and, changing his name to Paul, he harnessed the intellectual energy and the enthusiasm he had devoted to ruthless anti-Christian action to the conversion of the gentiles to Christianity. In the face of every difficulty—beatings by the Roman and Jewish authorities, stoning, shipwreck, attack by bandits, hunger, thirst and exposure, he made three long missionary journeys to Asia Minor and Europe (see map below) making converts and establishing new churches. His help to these young churches continued even after he, Paul, had left them, through his letters of advice and encouragement (included in the Epistles of the New Testament). Paul is portrayed on the frontispiece of a 14th-century Armenian manuscript of one of his Epistles (below left). He made two main contributions to Christianity. First, he established it firmly among the gentiles, in the framework of their own cultural traditions and customs, not forcing them to accept rigid Jewish laws as part of their faith. Second, he stressed the divinity of Christ, the redeemer who died for men's sins, Christ was divine, but he humbled himself and came to earth in human form to die and rise again for the sake of man. This concept of regeneration was very easily understood and accepted by the gentile nurtured on Greek mystery religions. In some ways Paul distorted the faith he had come to accept so dramatically. He taught that the human body was corrupt, as Christ never had. But it was Paul who first brought Christianity to the world, who widened its scope beyond the confines of a sect of orthodox Jews. Paul saw his mission as that of presenting Jesus to the people of the Hellenic world but it was his generosity to the church in Jerusalem that led to his death. He returned there with a collection for the poor and was mobbed and arrested. As a Roman citizen, he was able to insist on a trial in Rome and was kept in prison there until his death in A.D. 65. According to tradition he was buried, like Peter, in the catacombs in Rome (below center).

Below: map of the eastern Mediterranean shows the routes taken by Paul on his three great missionary journeys and also marks his last, when he was taken captive to Rome where he died.

First journey — — — —
Second journey ....
Third journey ————————
Final journey to Rome - - - - - - - - - -

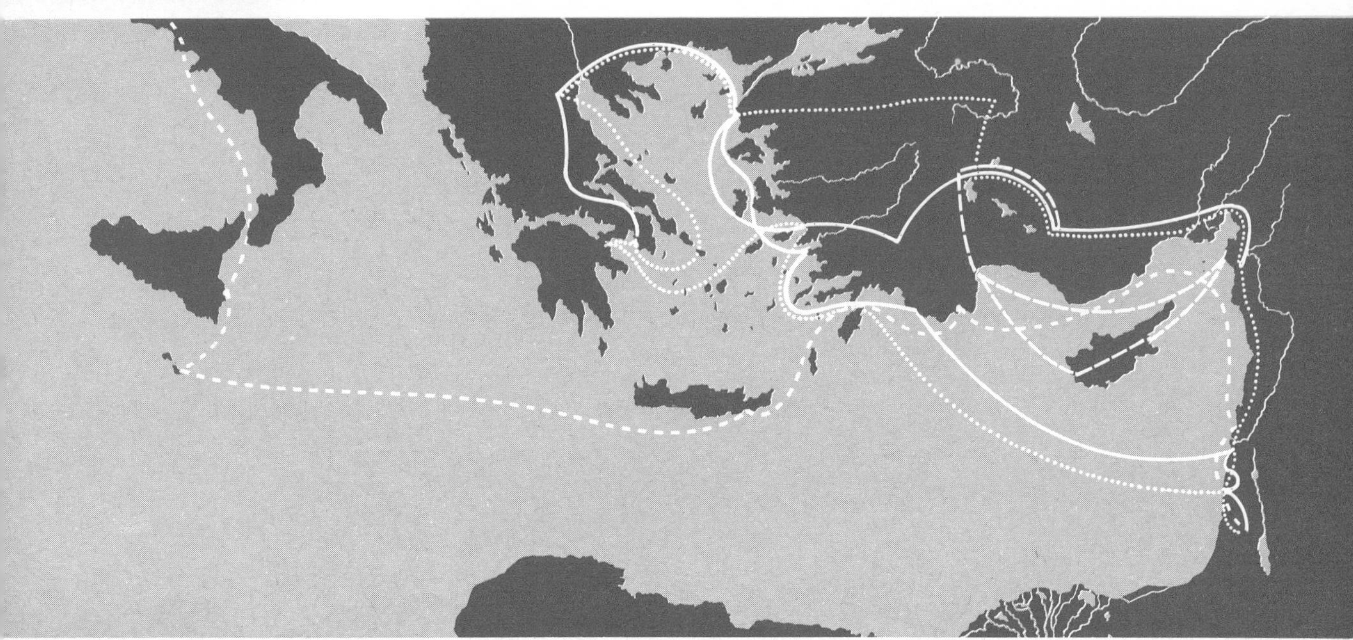

Above: the first Ecumenical Council at Nicaea (A.D. 325), called by the Emperor Constantine to settle doctrinal differences (16th-century Cretan painting), and which drew up the Nicene Creed. Below: demons attacking Christian souls ascending the heavenly ladder (12th-century icon). Origen, the early Christian philosopher, believed man ascended or descended through successive lives.

The First Centuries of the Church

During the three centuries after Paul's death, the Christian church faced many problems. Christians, scattered throughout the empire in areas of different languages and traditions, were more or less tolerated by the Romans for a time. They found converts in the Jewish quarters of the cities and among small tradespeople and slaves, many of whom were highly educated and generally obedient to Roman law. Unlike adherents of other cults and faiths permitted in the empire, however, Christians turned their backs on worldly power.

Christians aroused the suspicions of the common people because they often met privately and refused to recognize the divinity of the emperors, as the Jews had done. Rome tolerated the Jewish refusal to take an oath to the "genius" of the emperor and to participate in his official cult because they were basically one people in one land; but the Christians were spread in large numbers throughout the empire, and their refusal meant disloyalty and rebellion. So, although early Christians were not continually thrown to the lions, the authorities frequently made examples of them and the threat of persecution was always present. Its chief effect was to give even nonbelievers the impression that Christianity was worth dying for.

As the Goths, Visigoths and other northern barbarians became a real threat to Rome in the third century, every citizen of the empire was ordered to get a certificate from a government official affirming that he had sacrificed to the emperor's image, or be put to death. Christians refused and scorned those who lapsed or bribed officials to give them certificates without sacrificing. They were persecuted, tortured and killed in large numbers. Other persecutions followed, heavily and then sporadically, until the advent of Emperor Constantine in 324 (p. 54).

The character and organization of the Christian church were also changing. For one thing, the apostles and others who had actually known Jesus died as the congregations they founded grew. Their letters and sayings were collected to provide second-century believers with a record of their faith. By the end of the first century, it appears that most churches had developed an organization consisting of a superintendent (the Greek word

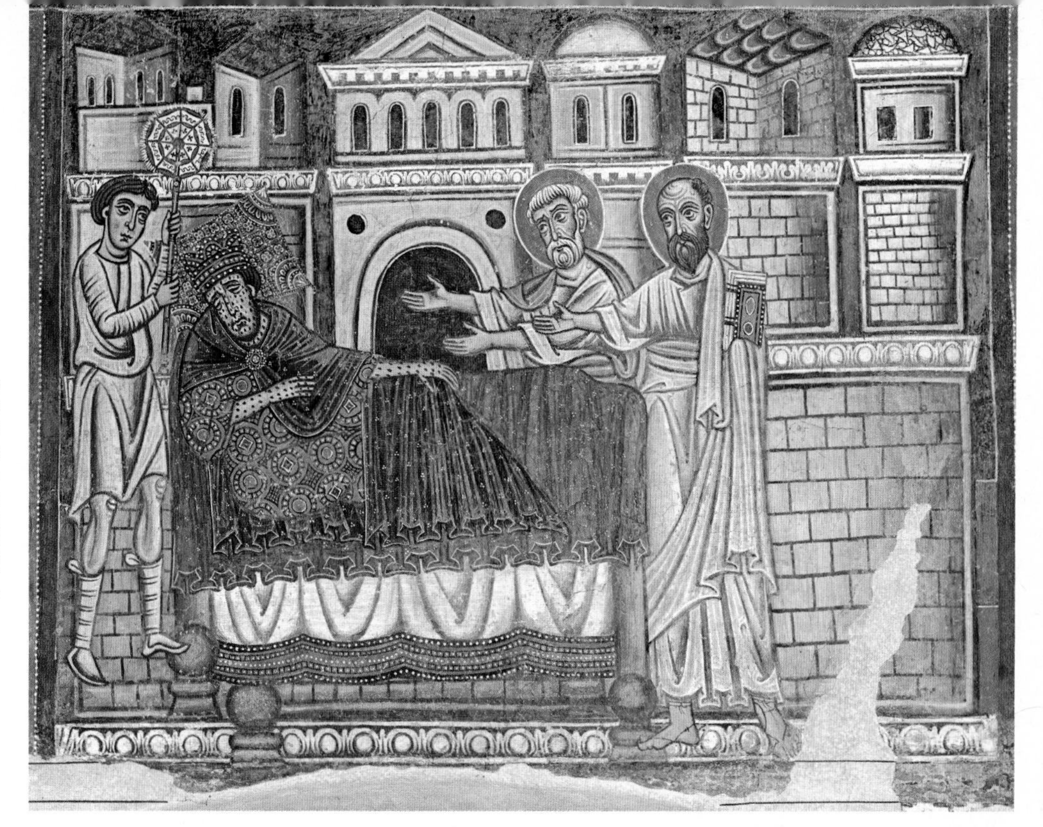

Right: the conversion of the Roman Emperor Constantine (about A.D. 312). Peter and Paul appeared to him in a dream and he saw a cross inscribed, "By this sign you shall conquer." Granting Christians recognition and freedom of worship, he ended 300 years of persecution.

episcopos is the root of bishop), a council of elders (or *presbyteroi*, from which the word priest comes), and stewards called *diaconi* (deacons). The principle of "apostolic succession" developed: As Peter and Paul had both gone to Rome, the church there came to be looked to for guidance, and bishops were believed to succeed to the apostles' authority by consecration.

A number of doctrinal questions arose from the different philosophical backgrounds of Christians, and the Church had to determine an orthodoxy for its believers as different sects developed and threatened its main body. By the second century, two deviations were widely honored. The first, Gnosticism (from the Greek *gnosis*, knowledge), held a dualistic view. The world, the body and matter generally were so vile that a good God could not have created them nor himself have become human. For the Gnostics, salvation lay in despising the body and cultivating knowledge through the spirit. The other great threat to orthodoxy was the Marcionite doctrine. Marcion denied the harsh, worldly God of the Old Testament and preached that only asceticism could bring man to the good God of the spirit who first revealed himself to Christ. And Christ, as the Son of God, could not be human, only divine.

In the East, Clement of Alexandria (about 150–215) taught that ignorance, not sin, was the chief cause of man's spiritual misery. His pupil Origen (p. 101) preached a doctrine of reincarnation and meditation. In the West, Tertullian (about 160–230, the first writer known to have used the expression "the Trinity") joined a group called the Montanists, who felt Christians should shut themselves off from the secular world. And everywhere Christian thinkers advanced conflicting theories about the nature of God, Jesus and the Holy Spirit, in an attempt to reconcile Christ's humanity with his divinity.

Below: Coptic rock church of St. George at Lalibella, Ethiopia. The early Church was divided by doctrinal disputes on the nature of Christ. The Egyptian sect of Coptic Christians believed that the human and the divine in Christ constituted one nature.

Definition and Dispute

Legend says that the Emperor Constantine (324–337) was converted to Christianity after he had a vision of the cross with the inscription *In hoc signo vinces* (By this sign you shall conquer). It is certain that when he became Emperor in 324 he stopped the persecutions, granted freedom of religion and tried to strengthen the church. As Christians formed about one sixth of the approximately 70 million people in the empire, their unity was important to the unity and stability of the empire itself. In 325 Constantine called a world council of churches at Nicaea, across the Bosporus from his new capital Constantinople, to put down the Arian heresy and others which were causing disputes. (The followers of Arius of Alexandria refused to believe that Christ was as divine as God.) The 300 bishops at Nicaea settled the controversies in what has become known as the Nicene Creed, which states that Christ is of the same substance as God the Father and the Holy Spirit.

Nevertheless, disputes about the nature of Jesus and the Incarnation continued. Nestorius of Antioch (died about 451) held that Christ was two separate personalities, one human and one divine. His contemporary, Cyril of Alexandria (376–444), argued that with a divine nature Christ could not choose evil and had not become truly man. He could not, therefore, truly redeem human nature. Apollinarius of Alexandria (310–390) argued a similar case. A second council at Chalcedon in 451 decided that Christ embodied two distinct but inseparable natures.

Perhaps the greatest Christian thinker of the time was St. Augustine (p. 104), who concerned himself less with the nature of Christ than with the problem of evil. He was converted to Christianity from Manicheanism. He became Bishop of Hippo, North Africa, and died while invading Vandals were besieging the city. In his writings, Augustine accepted the Trinity and developed the concepts of original sin and predestination which were to influence Catholics and Protestants for centuries. Man is bound by Adam's first sin to be born in sin, and only God's grace can save him. God's grace is a free gift to the undeserving; it cannot be earned, but the Church through its sacraments can provide the means of grace. A British monk, Pelagius (about 360–420), opposed Augustine, regarding Adam merely as a bad example and stressing faith as the justification for salvation, but Augustine's views were predominant.

By the time of the barbarian invasions of Italy in the fifth century, Rome and Constantinople had become seats of quite different churches. The Bishop of Rome, whose church was founded by St. Peter, had come to regard his place in the church hierarchy as supreme, basing his claim on apostolic succession. (In the middle of the second century, he had acquired the title of pope to distinguish his office.)

Constantinople, seat of the empire, held that it should be the seat of Christianity as well, and the rivalry was complicated by doctrinal disputes. For three centuries (from 589 to 876) the two churches argued over one phrase. Rome held that the Holy Spirit proceeds from the Father and the Son (in Latin *filioque*). Constantinople opposed *filioque*.

During the centuries of barbarian invasion, the popes had called for secular military aid. On Christmas Day 800, Charlemagne (768–814), whose father had kept the Lombard invaders out of Rome, was crowned Holy Roman Emperor by Pope Leo III. Official recognition of his title in Constantinople amounted to recognition of two empires. In 1054

Above: the interior of St. Sophia, Justinian's great Church of the Holy Wisdom in Constantinople. Now a museum, this Byzantine masterpiece was made a mosque when the Turks took Constantinople in 1453. Islamic embellishments in this view include the Sultan's box (left), the mihrab (prayer niche showing the direction of Mecca), the minber (pulpit) and large disks bearing the names of Allah, Mohammed and the first Caliphs and Imams.

Left: the second Council of Nicaea held in A.D. 787, at which the Emperor Constantine VI presided (center right), denounced iconoclasm (Greek for "image breaking") and made the veneration of holy pictures obligatory. This reversed an earlier emperor's decree abolishing image worship.

the Eastern and Western churches finally divided as a result of a dispute over papal jurisdiction. The Roman church called itself Catholic (universal), the church in Constantinople called itself Orthodox (right opinion). The Eastern Orthodox churches, in the Soviet Union and other Slavic countries as well as in Greece and parts of Asia Minor, have concerned themselves less with the intellect and the world than the Catholic church and have never suffered reformation. But while they remain unified, their identification with the tsars and other rulers led to their disestablishment and deliberate weakening in Communist countries.

Left: this iron Turkish helmet (15th century) from Constantinople is decorated with gold and silver and inscribed with a reference to the Moslem Mamluk rulers of Egypt.

Mohammed

Mohammed (570–632), the prophet who founded Islam, was born in Mecca, a city near the west coast of the Arabian Peninsula which lay at the center of trading routes between Asia and Europe. The city had another importance for the people who lived there or passed through it—the *Kaaba* (or cube), a square shrine incorporating an ancient meteorite. It housed idols of the principal desert nature deities—except for the vague chief god Allah—and was the goal of religious pilgrimages for centuries before the birth of Mohammed.

Mohammed, orphaned as a young child, grew up in the care of an uncle and grandfather who were trustees of the Kaaba and the sacred well near it. Mohammed married an older widow, Khadijah, and ran her caravan business successfully for years. Of their five children, only a daughter, Fatima, survived. They adopted Mohammed's first cousin Ali and a Christian slave boy Zaid. It seems clear that Mohammed was familiar, if perhaps a trifle inaccurately, with the basic tenets of Christianity and Judaism.

When about the age of 40, Mohammed went through a period of spiritual strain, worrying that the Day of Judgment might be at hand. His first religious visions made him fear for his sanity, and only Khadijah's comforting kept him from killing himself. More visions followed, clarifying his mission: Allah was the one God, and Mohammed his prophet. For years he was successful only in converting members of his own family. The citizens of Mecca were offended by his attacks on idolatry, which threatened the pilgrimages to Mecca and therefore their prosperity.

When Khadijah died and local hostility increased, Mohammed prepared to move to Yathrib, some 300 miles away. The city was torn by feuds and offered him hospitality if he could unite it. In 622, just as hostile Meccans were about to attack him, Mohammed made his famous flight *(hegira)* to

Left: 16th-century Turkish miniature depicting an event in the life of Mohammed. Here, he is given food by Christian monks while traveling on a caravan expedition to Syria. During the early part of his life Mohammed ran a caravan business in Mecca. Not until the age of 40 did he assume the role of the prophet of Allah.

Yathrib, which changed its name in his honor to Medina (the city of the prophet). In Medina, Mohammed established a theocracy. War with Mecca followed and in 630 Mohammed and his followers took the city. His first act was to pay homage to the sacred Kaaba before destroying its idols and establishing Mecca as the holy shrine of Islam.

The Islam (the word means submission, and Moslems are those who submit to the will of Allah) Mohammed preached was simple in its doctrine and the rules for its followers. Because the Koran, the holy book which Allah dictated to Mohammed, was written down the year after he died, Islam has never suffered the great textual disputes of other religions. Allah is the one omnipotent God who ordains everything, guiding men or leaving them to stray. He requires only submission to his will and observance of his rules, not penitence. When the final resurrection and Day of Judgment comes, the disobedient will be punished and the righteous will enter paradise, a garden of earthly delights and love.

Moslem worship takes place without pictures or music. Islam requires its followers to observe the simple legalistic duties outlined in the Koran and its uncomplicated moral code. Above all, Moslems are expected to follow the "five pillars" of the faith: (1) The Creed: There is no God but Allah and Mohammed is his prophet *(La ilah illa Allah, Muhammad rasul Allah)*. As this creed is basically the whole of the Moslem dogma, its importance has kept Mohammed himself from becoming an object of worship. (2) The Prayers: Specific prayers are said after washing five times a day. Believers face Mecca and repeat prescribed words and motions. (3) Alms: Money is given regularly for the poor and for upkeep of the mosques. During one period there is a war tax. (4) Fasting: During the month of Ramadan, when Mohammed received the Koran, Moslems fast from dawn until sunset. (5) The Pilgrimage: Every good Moslem should try to make at least one pilgrimage to Mecca.

The customs, organization and laws laid down in the Koran came to be supplemented by a collection of Mohammed's sayings, the *Hadith*. The Koran ensures a basic unity among various Moslem sects.

Above: the elaborately decorated dome of an Iranian mosque. The "five pillars" of the Moslem faith dictate that the believer shall give alms for the upkeep of mosques but he usually makes his formal daily prayers at home, facing in the direction of Mecca. Below: a Moslem cemetery near Ribat in Tunisia. The graves all lie parallel—the dead are buried on their right sides, facing Mecca.

The Extension of Islam

In the first century after Mohammed's death, Islam spread from the Pyrenees to the Himalayas—largely as a result of military conquest. From 630, when Mohammed and 10,000 men took Mecca by force, Islam unified desert tribes and townsmen militarily as well as religiously. The Prophet promised Moslems who fought with unbelievers four fifths of the booty if they survived, and a welcome in paradise if they lost their lives. The Christians of the Arabian Peninsula and the Persian and Byzantine empires were promised security and magnanimous treatment if they surrendered. Furthermore, most of them appreciated the strength of the conquerors and the relative simplicity of their doctrines, as well as the fact that the Koran recognizes Allah as the God of the Christians and Jews, and such figures as Abraham and Jesus as earlier prophets.

As the Arabs conquered more civilized parts of the world, their intellectual horizons expanded. Arab scholarship, influenced by Hellenistic science and philosophy, flourished. Although united by the Koran, Moslems disagreed about who should be the spiritual and temporal successors of Mohammed and two basic sects developed. The Shiites held that only descendants of Ali, the Prophet's son-in-law, could be caliph (successor). The majority group

Above: Palace of the Grand Masters of the Order of St. John at Rhodes. Christian knights held the island for two centuries against successive Turkish onslaughts but were driven out in 1522. Below: group of Moslems from Mogul India (18th-century miniature). Islam reached India in the eighth century. In 1340 a Turkish sultan ruled northern and central India; by the 17th century Moslem culture had penetrated all India except the extreme south.

of Sunnite Moslems denied this claim, and rival caliphs and interpretations led to a division of leadership and belief which still exists. In the eighth century another group of believers, called the Sufis after the coarse woolen robes they wore, practiced a mystical variety of Islam. Powerful, often militant, movements have developed in every century since Mohammed.

The conquests of Moslem Arabs and Turks were so extensive that Europe might have fallen to Islam if Charles Martel (714–741), grandfather of Charlemagne, had not kept them from overrunning France in the Battle of Tours in 732, and if they had not been defeated outside Vienna in the 16th and 17th centuries. Medieval Christians spent two centuries (1095–1291) fighting the Moslems for possession of the Holy Land. The chief effect appears to have been a politically vain sacrifice of lives, but the Crusades renewed contact and trade with the East. In the East, Moslem rule extended to India and what is now Indonesia, uniting its peoples through a shared religion and culture.

Today there are more than 300 million followers of Islam. They are concentrated in the Arab countries around the Mediterranean, and in Pakistan, Indonesia and Africa.

Above: Moslem women in the souk (bazaar) of Marrakesh, Morocco. Wearing veils is an Arab custom that dates from before the time of Mohammed. Moslem women, considered spiritually inferior to men, are subservient to their husbands, who alone may see them unveiled.

Below: the entrance to the 17th-century Mosque of the Barber at Kairouan in Tunisia, as it is today. Two pairs of shoes can be seen standing outside. Moslems must always remove their shoes, as a mark of respect, before entering a mosque.

Below: a cupola in the Alhambra, the palace of the Moslem Nasrid dynasty of Granada, Spain. When Granada fell in 1492 and the Christians drove the Moslems from southern Spain, they added the arms of Castile and Leon to the Moorish decoration of the cupola.

The Medieval Church and Monasticism

Above: the title page to the Gospel of St. Matthew in the Book of Kells, an early illuminated Bible executed in an Irish monastery. Below: another monastic treasure, a gilded wooden cross set with precious stones, from a monastery in Germany. As barbarian hordes poured across Europe, destroying the Roman Empire, much of its culture and scholarship was preserved in the monasteries where manuscripts were copied and libraries and schools established.

When Christianity became the state religion of the dying Roman Empire in the late fourth century, its character began to alter greatly. Paganism was discouraged by the state, even mildly persecuted, and the devoted Christian minority swelled to a less devout majority. Identified with the state, the Church took on many of its trappings. The Church also began to accumulate great wealth. As hordes of barbarians invaded from the north, bringing about the dissolution of the empire, the Church stood firm while temporal territories and powers changed hands. The popes of the Dark Ages and the Middle Ages were almost always engaged in struggles with emperors and other rulers; and as the papal concerns appeared increasingly worldly, the Christian monastic tradition developed.

Earlier, particularly in areas where the Eastern Orthodox Church predominated, individual men had withdrawn from the world to practice solitary meditation, partly in imitation of Christ's 40 days in the wilderness and partly under the influence of Eastern asceticism and contemporary cults which condemned the body as corrupt. Some went to the eccentric extreme of installing themselves on top of pillars to escape the contamination of the world. Others joined communities shut off from the world by a wall (or *claustrum*, from which the word cloister comes), living simply, meditating and praying.

As the temporal effectiveness (or corruption) of the Church increased, many devout Christians were attracted to monasticism as a way of preserving and increasing sanctity. In the sixth century, Benedict of Nursia (about 480–543) founded a monastery at Monte Cassino with rules which checked any trend to extremes of asceticism and became a model for many others. Under the motto of *ora et labora* (pray and work), the Benedictine rules required permanent residence and vows of chastity and obedience. Members of the order lived a simple life of work in the monastery fields and workshops, worship and prayer during the day and part of the night, and serious reading. Benedictine monasteries were founded all over Europe.

Right: medallions decorating this manuscript depict the four Mendicant Orders: Dominicans, Carmelites, Franciscans and Augustinians. They felt it their mission to renew religious faith by living and preaching among the poor.

Below: the Monastery of Stavrovoumi, Cyprus. Its situation is typical of the sites of early monasteries whose founders felt that physical isolation brought spiritual isolation from the base and contaminating influences of the world.

In the 13th century Francis of Assisi (about 1182–1226) formed a less intellectual order whose members took an additional vow of poverty. Franciscans went out into the world to minister to the forgotten and the unfortunate. The Dominicans began as missionaries. They originally begged for their daily food and, as well as being sent to convert heretics in southern France, went about preaching.

Historically, perhaps the greatest achievement of the monastic orders was to preserve learning and culture. It was in the monasteries of the Dark and Middle Ages that manuscripts were carefully copied. Educated monks and priests served as advisers to kings and princes, many of whom could scarcely write their own names. Missionary monks told the stories of Christianity to the ordinary people. Monasteries collected libraries and housed schools in a period when Greek and Roman culture had been destroyed or almost forgotten during the barbarian invasions.

The monastic orders also produced men who took Christian theology and philosophy further. Educated Irish monks traveled throughout Europe. An intellectual (but for the Church more than intellectual) dispute, over whether the communion bread and wine are really transformed into the actual body and blood of Christ, caused the 13th-century Pope Innocent III (1198–1216) to lead the Fourth Lateran Council to make transubstantiation (miraculous transformation into Christ's body and blood) a dogma of the church.

Scholastic monks grappled with the teachings of Aristotle when they were recovered in the 12th century. One of those who studied Aristotle's natural science was Thomas Aquinas (p. 110), a 13th-century Italian Dominican friar. Aquinas taught and studied in Paris and Cologne. He produced a synthesis of faith and philosophy amounting to a new theology in his two great works, *Summa Contra Gentiles* and *Summa Theologica*.

Above: the nave of Exeter Cathedral, built in the second half of the 14th century. Today it is one of the finest examples of Gothic architecture in England. Such magnificence was deliberately created as a visual reminder of the power of God in an age of illiteracy.

Right: 13th-century ivory statue of the Virgin Mary opens to reveal a triptych of scenes from her life (except center right panel, Pentecost), from the annunciation to her coronation in heaven.

The Church and the Common Man

Christians of the Middle Ages and the early Renaissance lived at a time when the prevailing view of the world was a religious one. Even if a man was not religious himself, the world around him was, at least apparently. God was the supreme authority, the Church his agent on earth and (in theory) temporal rulers derived their authority from God and the Church. This hierarchy continued through the social and political scale. Life was hard, but the man who could escape sin or be truly penitent when he lapsed would achieve salvation after death.

By the fifth century, the Church had established the practice of regular and private confession. Local priests were the chief source of moral instruction for their parishioners—who included almost everyone. The instruction was chiefly by practice: the Lord's Prayer, the Hail Mary, regular attendance at Sunday Mass and the obligatory annual communion after confession at Easter. Mass was said in Latin, with almost no participation by the community, and local priests and traveling friars preached sermons.

Because the constant temptation to sin and forego salvation pervaded ordinary religious belief, evil forces, devils and witches were feared. It became common for people to pray to Mary, the mother of Jesus, or to the saints for intercession with God for the gift of grace. Bodily remains of the saints were put in precious cases and venerated, and great value was attached to pilgrimages to holy places.

The Church was very wealthy. Individual churches and monasteries owned and managed vast areas of land all over Europe. Beautiful churches, the most magnificent buildings of their time, were built everywhere and filled with precious paintings and statues. It is difficult for a person born in the 20th century to imagine, for example, the effect of the grandeur of Chartres Cathedral on a devout medieval peasant whose own life was very poor. The Church was also, in part, corrupt. It was possible to buy ecclesiastical office (simony) and to arrange religious position for a member of the family (nepotism). The Church was often generous with its wealth, however, taking in the needy and homeless and ministering to the sick.

Few Christians could hope to become educated or to become monks or priests, but the example of the medieval mystics provided another way to

sanctity. Many of the well-known mystics were highly-educated men who contributed to religious and philosophical discussion about the way to God. Thomas à Kempis (about 1379–1471) produced a work, the *Imitation of Christ*, which has helped many to a closer knowledge of God and Jesus.

In the 14th century, the way to Protestantism was paved by John Wycliffe (about 1320–84), a professor of theology at Oxford, who challenged the right of the decaying Church hierarchy to rule without divine grace. Holding the Bible to be the only true authority on matters of belief, he denied the doctrine of transubstantiation. He translated the Bible into English and sent his Lollard priests to teach the Bible in English to ordinary people. Wycliffe was condemned as a heretic posthumously, but before he died he influenced John Huss (about 1369–1415) in Bohemia. Huss led a popular revolt so powerful that he was condemned to death at the Council of Constance in 1415. The 15th-century councils at Constance and Basle were more immediately successful in putting down dissenters than in reforming the Church. But as France and England grew more independent, papal power waned.

Above: incense burning for pagans on the steps of the parish church at Chichicastenango in Guatemala, where Christian converts still retain some of their earlier pagan beliefs.
Below: a procession in Seville, Spain, during Easter week. The masked figures represent repentant sinners whose identities are concealed.

CHRISTIANITY DIVIDED

In western Europe, the Roman Catholic Church influenced every aspect of life in the Middle Ages. Corruption increased, and ultimately Luther and Calvin broke away from the Church and Protestantism emerged. Reforms within the Catholic Church failed to reunite Christians. In following centuries, Christianity splintered further and faced the challenge of science. Today, Christianity is again going through a period of reappraisal and attempts at reconciliation in the face of religious apathy and the uncertainty of a nuclear world.

Pope Paul VI in St. Patrick's Cathedral, New York City on October 4, 1965. On the same day he spoke before the UN "for the cause of peace in the world." Divided since the Reformation, Catholics and Protestants today are drawing closer together to face the problems of the modern world.

Protestantism: Luther and Calvin

The division of the Church into Catholic and Protestant can be dated: October 31, 1517, when the Augustinian monk Martin Luther (1483–1546) nailed his 95 theses to the door of a church in Wittenberg. The theses were an attack on the practice of selling papal indulgences (a system under which people purchased remission of temporal punishment for sins). Although Luther apparently did not mean them to be the first steps in the founding of a new church, the way in which his attack was received by the Church and by other dissidents led inexorably to the Reformation. Luther who had long wrestled privately with the problems of guilt and salvation, refused to recant, supporting his stand with the word of God in the Bible. His temporal superior, Frederick, the elector of Saxony (1486–1525), protected him from the Church's ban on sheltering him or reading his works.

Luther married a former nun and raised a family. He translated the Bible into German, making the scriptures available in ordinary language. His hymnbook gave the congregation more participation in the service than they had enjoyed before.

Luther's Christianity had a wide and powerful appeal. Respect for the Catholic Church was rapidly declining as a result of its internal corruption, and the middle class was becoming used to thinking for itself. Certain German princes who expected to profit politically from the Church's weakness encouraged dissent.

Although Luther accepted many elements of Catholic belief and practice, his two basic convictions made reconciliation impossible. The scriptures, not bishops and priests, form the final religious authority for every Christian; indeed every man is spiritually competent enough to be a potential priest. The justification of God's grace lies in faith, not good works (and indulgences). The man who is a true believer will naturally live a life of

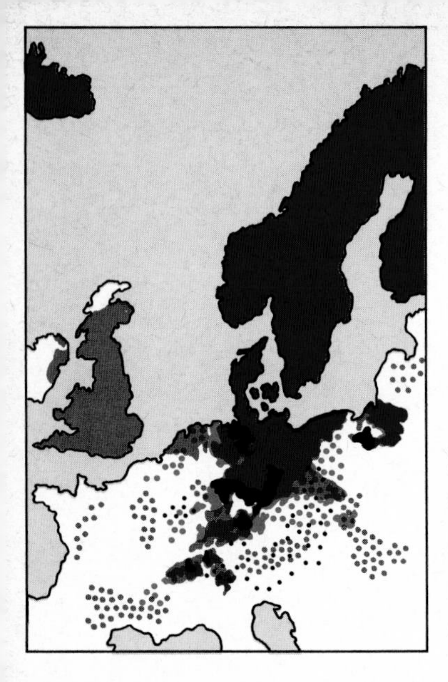

Left: a map illustrating the spread of Protestantism in 16th-century Europe. Black areas show the extent of the movement in 1529. By 1555 it covered most of Germany and Scandinavia (red). By 1600 it had reached the Low Countries and Britain (gray) from which it spread to North America.

good works. The princely states of Germany were racked for decades by struggles between Lutherans and the Church, although Luther himself ordered Lutherans to obey state authorities. With the Peace of Augsburg in 1555, a compromise was reached: *cujus regio, ejus religio* (whoever rules the area determines the religion).

Martin Luther did not leave a precise theology, and his own religion was essentially conservative. The more radical reformation in Switzerland gave Protestantism the features which still distinguish it from Catholicism. Before 1530, Ulrich Zwingli (1484–1531), a parish priest in Zurich, had denounced the doctrine of transubstantiation. He persuaded congregations to minimize ritual and govern themselves, practicing only what is commanded in the Bible.

By the time Zwingli died in a battle between Catholic and Reformed forces, his teachings had been absorbed by John Calvin (1509–64). Calvin, a second-generation Protestant, fled to Geneva from France, where he had just published an uncompromisingly harsh definition of the Protestant

Above: *The Fishers for Souls* by van de Velde (1636–72), an allegory on Catholic-Protestant conflict. It shows the Netherlands divided between Catholics (right) and Protestants (left) during the 1609–21 truce in the religious wars. Opposing clergy (center) continue the spiritual war for men's souls.

Below: contemporary engraving shows 16th-century "heroes" of Europe's Protestant movement. Martin Luther, Germany (center left), and John Calvin, Switzerland, were the acknowledged leaders. Scotland's John Knox sits at the right with pen poised.

position, *The Institutes of the Christian Religion.* For Calvin there were a number of basic truths: (1) God is omnipotent and inscrutable. All he does is good, even if human beings fail to understand. (2) Man's understanding of God is weakened by original sin. The Bible is his source of revelation. (3) By original sin, men are corrupt and deserve to be condemned before the sight of God. (4) Some men are saved through justification by faith—if God chooses to save them. (5) Those who are saved are predestined to their salvation. (6) There is no justification by works, but those whom God elects to save abound in good works, and their righteousness is evidence of their salvation.

Calvin established a theocracy in Geneva, and the city drew refugee Protestant scholars from all over Europe, including John Knox (about 1510–72). Knox returned to Scotland, where in 1560 the Scottish parliament ratified what came to be called the Presbyterian Church as the state church of Scotland. By the end of the 17th century, Protestants had become the dominant religious force in Britain, Scandinavia, America and northern Germany.

Protestant church in Port Washington, Long Island, New York. The simplicity of the architecture reflects the desire to simplify the ritual of the church, based on the Protestant doctrine of freedom of worship within the authority of the Bible. This reliance on private judgment and the Bible has led to the great variety of sects.

The Counter Reformation

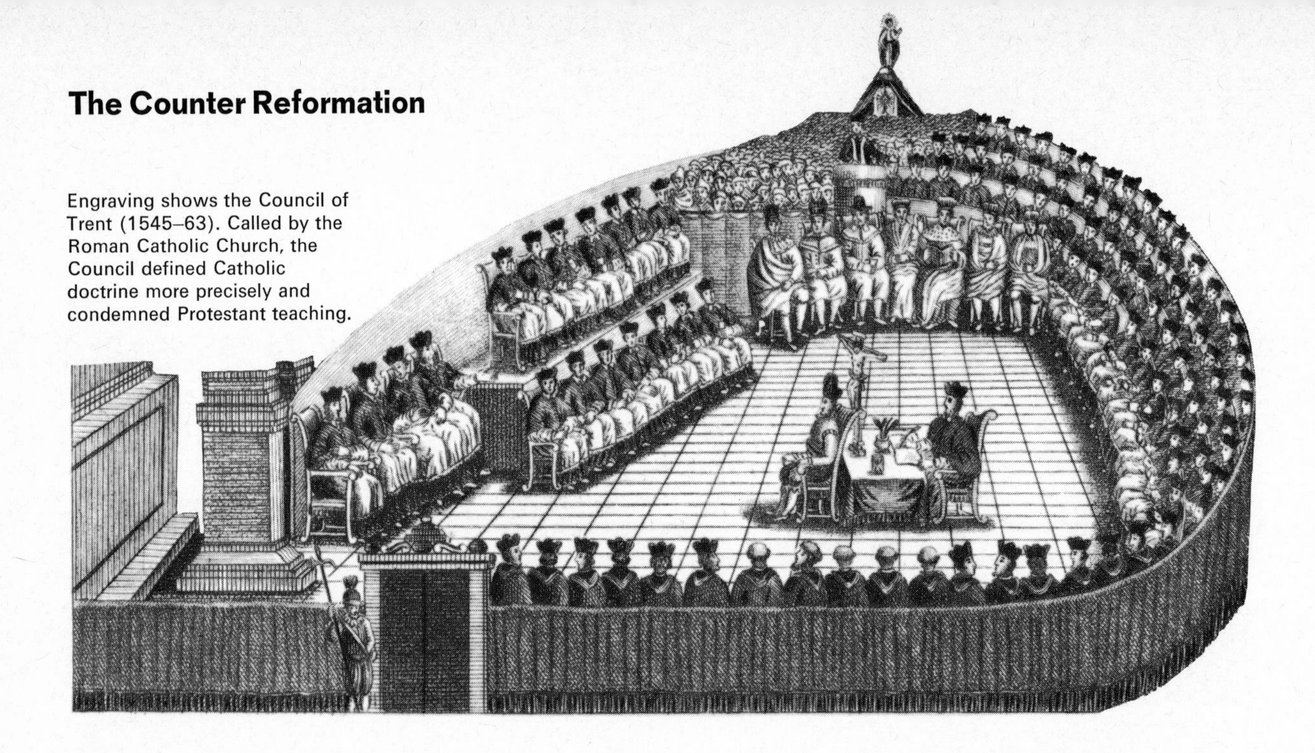

Engraving shows the Council of Trent (1545–63). Called by the Roman Catholic Church, the Council defined Catholic doctrine more precisely and condemned Protestant teaching.

Even before the threat of Protestantism arose, Roman Catholics were urging reform within the Church. By the time Luther published his 95 theses, Cardinal Jiménez (1436–1517) had instituted reforms in Spain. Italian priests and laymen were beginning to purge their church as well. English scholars like John Colet (about 1467–1519) and Sir Thomas More (1478–1535) were urging Rome to purify the Church as a whole. But although the seeds of self-criticism had been planted before Luther and Calvin, it was the popularity of their Christianity which gave the Catholic Church the impetus for the Counter Reformation.

After efforts at reunification failed, Emperor Charles V (1519–56) persuaded Pope Paul III (1534–49) to call the Council of Trent in 1545. It met intermittently until 1563 to redefine the Catholic position and correct ecclesiastical abuses. The Council cut back on the issuing of indulgences and the veneration of saints, reduced the number of holy days in the year, and established an Index of prohibited books to limit the spread of Protestant propaganda. The Council further encouraged bishops and priests to teach their congregations more about the scriptures and Catholicism.

The five basic positions taken by the Council made compromise with the Protestants impossible: (1) The Calvinist conviction of predestination and the Lutheran doctrine of justification by faith were condemned. Justification may be by faith, but it rests on good works as well. (2) Only the Catholic Church has the right to interpret the scriptures. (3) The Latin translation of the Bible, the *Vulgate*, is the sacred authorized version of the scriptures. (4) Catholic tradition has equal weight with the scriptures as a source of spiritual truth and moral conduct. (5) The sacraments recognized by the Protestants (baptism and communion) are only two of seven—baptism, confirmation, communion, penance, marriage, holy orders and extreme unction. The Council of Trent also affirmed the doctrine of transubstantiation and encouraged the establishment of seminaries for training priests.

Left: Ignatius of Loyola (1491–1556), founder of the Society of Jesus, presenting a book to Pope Paul III (1534–49). Loyola inspired great crusading zeal in his early followers, intelligent and disciplined men ready to challenge Protestant reformers.

Those who lapsed were encouraged to confirm allegiance to Rome by the revival of the Inquisition, which had operated chiefly in Spain during the 15th century. New monastic orders arising out of the Counter Reformation provided a milder way of encouraging the faith, and among them the Jesuits were outstanding.

Ignatius of Loyola (1491–1556) was a Spanish nobleman. He devoted himself to religious literature while recovering from serious battle wounds. His reading convinced him to become a "knight of the Virgin," and he hung his weapons over her altar at Montserrat and entered a Dominican monastery. After further study and spiritual exercises with his friends, Loyola offered his services and theirs directly to the pope. Loyola founded the Society of Jesus in 1534 and the pope approved it in 1540. Disciplined by spiritual exercises, Jesuits took an oath of absolute obedience and commitment. Certain about the basic rightness of their cause, they sanctioned "mental reservation"—a doubtful course of action may be followed if its goal is good.

The diligence and discipline of the Jesuits led to spectacular missionary successes, like those of St. Francis Xavier (1506–52) in the Far East and the priests who went to North, Central and South America in the 16th and 17th centuries. Jesuits also helped to check Protestantism in southern Germany and were powerful political influences in other countries.

The Counter Reformation never overcame the challenge of Protestantism, but it checked its spread.

Above: a painting by the Spanish artist, Alfonso Berraguete (1486–1561), illustrates the *auto da fé* (act of faith) which ended sessions of the Inquisition. This ceremony culminated in a sermon on the sin of heresy before sentence was passed on the guilty.

Below: *St. Bartholomew's Day Massacre*, painting by a Huguenot who survived the butchery. On August 24, 1572, Protestants in Paris were hunted down and more than 2,000 were killed. This news spread quickly to the French provinces where similar massacres followed.

Protestant Division

As the Roman Catholic Church consolidated itself, the Protestants divided still further. Britain's Parliament disassociated the Church of England from Rome, which had refused to give the heirless Henry VIII a divorce so that he could remarry. The king, not the pope, became head of the English Church. But the beliefs of the Church of England lay closer to Rome than to radical Protestantism, and Puritan reforming strains developed which tried to eliminate all reminders of the Catholic past. These religious differences helped to widen the rift between King Charles I and Parliament, and civil war broke out in 1640. The engraving (bottom left) shows Puritan iconoclasts who often broke into churches pulling down "popish" pictures and breaking statuary. In 16th-century Spain, a more tranquil side to the Counter Reformation was the revival of mysticism, a belief which encourages withdrawal from secular concerns. On the opposite page is Bernini's statue of St. Teresa of Avila (1515–82), an ardent mystic who, with St. John of the Cross, reformed the Carmelite order of nuns. Early in the 17th century, the Baptist movement arose from the Anabaptists who opposed infant baptism. Fiercely persecuted, the Anabaptists were dispersed throughout Europe. John Smyth founded the first Baptist church in England in 1612 and, in 1639, a group founded a church on Rhode Island. The Quakers, or Society of Friends, like the Baptists, rejected formalism and preferred to worship in their own homes. George Fox, their founder, believed that real "concern," illumination by an inner light, is the basis of true Christianity. The 19th-century watercolor (top left) shows a typical Quaker meeting. In the mid-18th century, another movement to reform the Church from within gave rise to a further form of Protestantism. This group, which included John Wesley (center left), became known as "Methodists," and their open-air teaching converted so many people that separation from the established Church soon became inevitable.

Deists and Skeptics

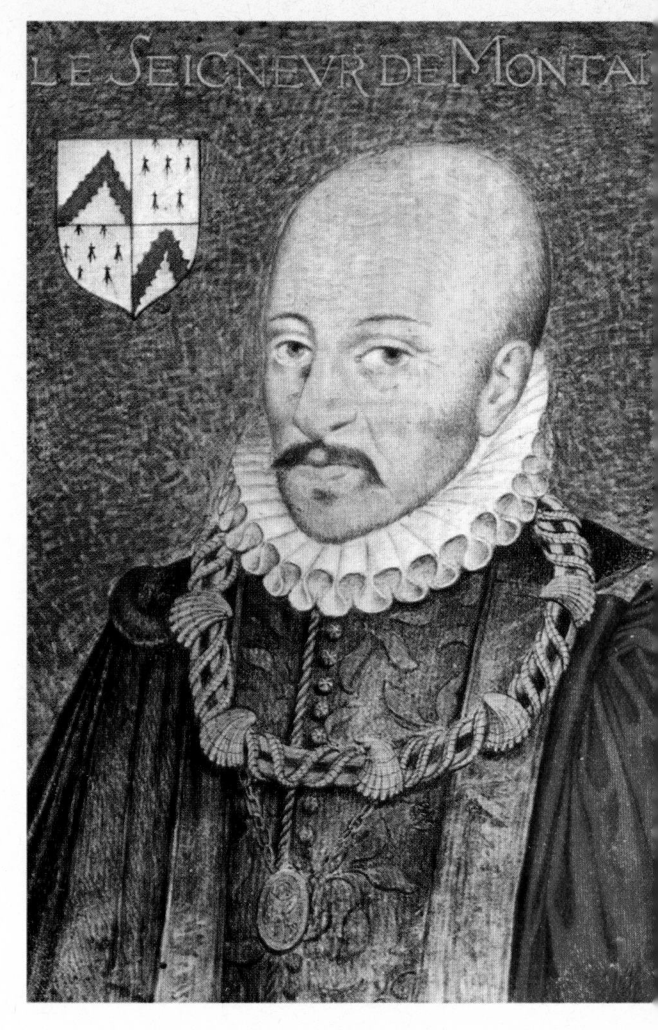

During the 16th and 17th centuries, Protestantism produced a series of religious controversies. As new interpretations of Christianity first encouraged individual believers and then hardened into formal doctrines, further splintering continued. Parallel to the often contradictory beliefs of enthusiastic extremes, fresh attempts were made to reach basic and universal theological truths. Developments in natural science and philosophy encouraged theological thinkers to use new methods. They began to emphasize observation and reason, and the principle of doubt formulated by René Descartes (p. 118).

Among thoughtful Christians, doubt about such things as the miracles related in the Bible was natural. The observable natural laws of science in God's own universe denied them. In some cases, notably the Church of England, a fair degree of skepticism was tolerated. Latitudinarian bishops permitted intellectual hostility to the supernatural elements of Christianity in a religion based on a distant God and good conduct. (It was in part the aridity of this kind of faith which gave the warmth and emotionalism of Methodism its great appeal.)

Although scientists like Robert Boyle (1627–91) and Sir Isaac Newton (p. 116) were believers, they looked for law in nature, not God, and the nature of God came under examination. The Deists limited God. Five basic points were developed by Lord Herbert of Cherbury (1583–1648): (1) there is a God; (2) men ought to worship him; (3) men can worship him chiefly by living a good life; (4) it is man's duty to repent when he sins; (5) there is

Above: Michel de Montaigne (1533–92), a French philosopher of Jewish descent. Doubting the validity of human knowledge, Montaigne arrived at skepticism composed of humility and universal goodwill.

Below: an engraving of Voltaire (1694–1778) talking to Frederick II of Prussia (left). Although a Deist, Voltaire derided the evil in the world, rejected miracles and challenged the authority of the Bible.

Right: Lord Herbert of Cherbury, the first Deist.
Below: frontispiece designed in 1764 for Diderot's *Encyclopédie*. The Encyclopedists upheld enlightenment attained through reason rather than revelation.

another life of punishments and rewards to come.

Later Deists, like John Toland (1670–1722) and Matthew Tindal (about 1655–1733), stressed the role of pure reason in religion, arguing that revelation could only confirm what is known by reason. In the 18th-century Age of Enlightenment, God was regarded as outside the universe. Deists believed that God created the universe and then left it to run without interference. Religion consisted of observing the fatherhood of God and brotherhood of man. By separating God from his universe—which, made by God and subject to spectacularly regular laws, must be perfect—they avoided a serious clash between religion and science.

Deist beliefs were crushingly answered by serious orthodox arguments. In *Alciphron* (1732), Bishop George Berkeley (p. 124) questioned the Deistic assumption of a division between the physical and spiritual by arguing that what a man perceives is not necessarily the most real. And Bishop Joseph Butler (1692–1752) published a telling argument for orthodox Christianity in his *Analogy of Religion* (1737): The fact that some aspects of the universe obey orderly natural laws does not mean that everything does, because man's own experience reveals inconsistencies.

In England, France and elsewhere in Europe, skeptics interested themselves in "natural religion," that was common to all men. Denis Diderot (p. 128) and the other skeptics who published the famous *Encyclopédie* rejected Christian revelation for the simplicity of natural religion. The German philosopher and playwright Gotthold Lessing (1729–81) defended religion as such; but in works like his great drama of tolerance, *Nathan the Wise*, he denied that any particular creed has an exclusive monopoly on religious truth. The savage attacks of Voltaire (1694–1778) on the "perfect world" of some Deists and the supernatural claims of Christianity encouraged further skepticism about the problem of world evil.

In the 19th century, the challenge of science had to be met head on. Christian scholars earnestly searched for the sources of the Bible, in an attempt to separate myth from revelation. The evolutionary theories Charles Darwin (1809–82) developed in *The Origin of Species* (1859) shattered orthodox ideas about creation and the special nature of man, and led to a conflict between religion and science which is still not resolved.

Missionary Expansion

One of the first Christian missionaries, St. Paul undertook many dangerous journeys to carry the new faith into Asia Minor. So began the first great missionary era when early Christians spread their faith all over Europe. From the Dark Ages through the Middle Ages to the Reformation there was comparatively little missionary work in the Western Church since most of the Western world was already loosely united in a Christian empire. After the Reformation Protestants were more concerned with consolidating their beliefs than with missionary work. But the Counter Reformation produced a burst of activity among Catholics, especially the Jesuits, who did not confine their missionary zeal to Europe.
The greatest of these missionaries was St. Francis Xavier (1506–52) whose kindness and patience won him thousands of converts in India, China and Japan. The Japanese screen painting (below left) shows Portuguese Jesuits landing in Japan. The Jesuits were outstandingly successful in Latin America under Portuguese and Spanish control. But here traditional religions still persist mingled with Christianity. The picture (top left) shows a head representing a pagan religion and a cross standing side-by-side on a hill-top near Chichicastenango, Guatemala. The third great burst of missionary activity came during the 19th century in Africa with colonial expansion and improved methods of transportation and communication. Here, too, old religions died hard. A West African Ibo mud sculpture of Christ as a schoolboy (top right) adorns the shrine of Ala, the Ibo earth goddess. Today missionaries of all denominations have extended the scope of their work to include medicine and education. This Seventh Day Adventist mission school on Lake Titicaca, Peru (below right) belongs to a new sect developed in the 19th century. Seventh Day Adventists preach in almost 800 languages and dialects.

Later Sects

Above: Salvation Army tambourinists. William Booth, a former Methodist minister, founded the Salvation Army in London in 1878. This semi-military evangelical and social service organization now operates all over the world. "Officers" in uniform conduct open-air meetings, presenting the gospel in the popular idiom.

The attempts made in the 18th and 19th centuries to sort out the relationship between religion and science led, on the one hand, to both austere and emotional reform movements in established Protestant churches and, on the other, to a number of concepts of God and man. Some of these conceptions were influenced by increased knowledge of other religions, others by a belief that religion must be concerned with the human social condition and improvements in the quality of life on this earth.

Some groups based their Christianity on Christ's Second Coming, although their other beliefs were quite different. In England, John Thomas (1805–71) founded a group called the Christadelphians. They interpreted the scriptures literally and believed that divine intervention in world affairs was imminent. The Church of Jesus Christ of Latter-day Saints, better known as the Mormons, was founded by Joseph Smith (1805–44), who in 1823 found the *Book of Mormon* after its existence was revealed to him in a vision. In 1847, Smith's successor, Brigham Young (1801–77), led some 4,000 followers to Utah where they founded Salt Lake City which became their headquarters.

Some aspects of Mormonism are taken from traditional Christianity, but some beliefs and practices differ. Mormon belief in eternal life makes it possible to baptize by proxy people who have died. Man is believed to possess a soul which existed in the presence of God before this life and will continue to live afterwards, and the earth is seen as a testing place, where man can prove his faithfulness to God's laws even when separated from the divine presence. Many Mormons are active in their communities, and young Mormons are encouraged to spend some time as missionaries.

Other groups have concerned themselves with the occult. The Swedenborgians were founded by the 18th-century Swedish scientist and mathemati-

The great Mormon Temple in Salt Lake City, Utah, center of the Church of Jesus Christ of Latter-day Saints. Built 1853–93, it is used only by Mormons. Open to the general public, Mormon meeting houses have facilities for study, recreation and worship. Mormons claim both spiritual and lineal descent from the tribes of Israel.

Founders of new sects which emerged in the 19th century. Joseph Smith (1805–44), who founded the Mormon Church. Theosophist Madame E. P. Blavatsky who upheld the Upanishadic revelations. Mary Baker Eddy (1821–1910), founder of Christian Science. Rudolf Steiner (1861–1925), the German theosophist and philosopher who developed anthroposophy. Steiner held that man could exercise his spiritual powers to acquire knowledge of "higher worlds."

Joseph Smith

Madame E. P. Blavatsky

Mary Baker Eddy

Rudolf Steiner

cian Emmanuel Swedenborg (1688–1772). They base their belief on an ordinarily unseen "real world" (although Swedenborg said he had visions of it), of which the world man lives in is a parallel. The Theosophists denied the existence of a personal god and personal immortality, affirming the transmigration of souls. Their founder, Madame Blavatsky (1831–91), upheld the revelations of the Hindu *Upanishads* (p. 26) and set up headquarters in India. Concern for a spiritual world and the state of man after death has also led to the fusion of Christianity and spiritualism, although orthodox Christianity has generally been highly skeptical about communication with the dead.

Christian Science emphasizes power of the mind and spirit. Mary Baker Eddy (1821–1910), who founded the First Church of Christ, Scientist, in Boston in 1879, taught that only the mind and spirit were real. What appeared to be a physical reality—the body, for example—was only an illusion, and exercise of faith and the mind could make physical ills disappear.

Two superficially less spiritual groups have had great impact, especially in Engish-speaking countries. The Young Men's Christian Association (and the YWCA), started in London in 1844, and the Salvation Army. The Ys, broadly nonsectarian, have made an unmistakable contribution to Christian fellowship among young people. The Salvation Army, founded by William Booth (1829–1912) in 1878, is rooted in Methodism, and organized on military lines. Booth originally preached simply to the uneducated, but the movement has developed into a wide-ranging and effective instrument of social aid, without losing its strongly Christian content.

British spiritualist healer Harry Edwards at a public demonstration of his healing powers held in Leeds, Yorkshire, in 1964. Here he treats a patient by "laying on of hands."

Another patient prays as the aid of a spirit is invoked to cure her. With the help of spirit guides, Harry Edwards claims to have healed about 10,000 patients in four years.

Modern Orthodoxy

Above: cartoon of Charles Darwin from *Vanity Fair* (1871). Published in 1859, Darwin's *The Origin of Species* led to a bitter struggle between Darwinians and Christians of all denominations, since his principle of evolution refuted the Bible's story of the creation.

Dwight L. Moody (1837–99), on the left, American evangelist, with Ira D. Sankey, the hymn writer and gospel singer, at a revival meeting in Brooklyn. Although not a trained theologian, Moody's teachings were in line with those of the orthodox churches. He also founded the interdenominational Moody Memorial Church.

Several aspects of the Roman Catholic Church's description of itself have made its history since the Reformation different from the course taken by Protestantism: It is apostolic, holy and catholic. It is apostolic because its priests and bishops are believed to derive their authority from the apostles; holy because its doctrines and sacraments lead men to salvation as an instrument of redemption; and catholic because it forms the only holy way for all men to achieve salvation. Because there can be no true salvation outside the Church, Rome has had to come to terms with historical developments and yet cannot change its basic nature by extreme compromise, lest it deny the validity of its past.

Two major doctrinal changes in the 19th century widened the gap between Rome and the Protestant churches. In 1854 Pope Pius IX (1846–78) proclaimed the doctrine of the Immaculate Conception of the Virgin Mary, and in 1870 the doctrine of Papal Infallibility. The latter does not mean that the Pope is never wrong, but that what he says *ex cathedra* (from the chair, or speaking as the pope) is the "revelation of faith delivered through the apostles," and thus binding on all Catholics. The controversies arising from the late 19th-century discoveries in science and biblical scholarship could not be easily assimilated against this background. In a general sense, Catholics of a speculative nature had to be either right or wrong.

The 19th-century biographies of Christ by Ernest Renan (1823–92) and David Friedrich Strauss (1808–74) attempted to show Jesus as a figure acceptable to modern, scientific man. Biblical history was widely said to be chiefly Jewish mythology. The theories of Albrecht Ritschl (1822–89) divorced faith and metaphysics, justifying Christianity as an ethical response to the life and teachings of Jesus and rejecting mysticism and mystery as deception.

All of these theological speculation posed the threat that if the Church compromised and adopted

Right: Vatican Council II, the twenty-first Ecumenical Council, opened in the Vatican City, Rome on October 11, 1962. Although the twentieth council of 1869 had widened the gap between Catholics and Protestants, Vatican II proclaimed that all men have the right to religious freedom but maintained Catholicism was the true faith.

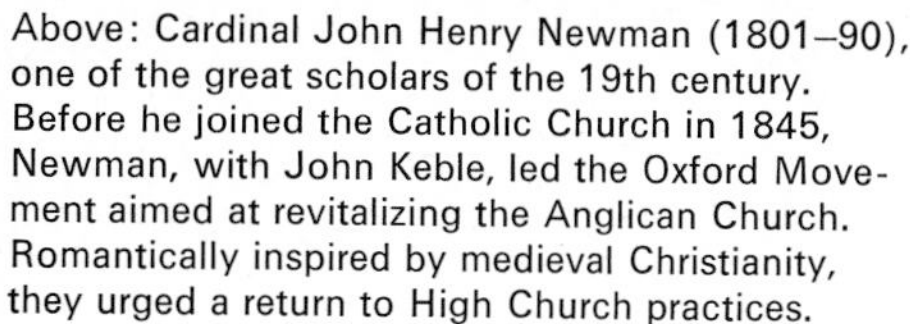

Above: Cardinal John Henry Newman (1801–90), one of the great scholars of the 19th century. Before he joined the Catholic Church in 1845, Newman, with John Keble, led the Oxford Movement aimed at revitalizing the Anglican Church. Romantically inspired by medieval Christianity, they urged a return to High Church practices.

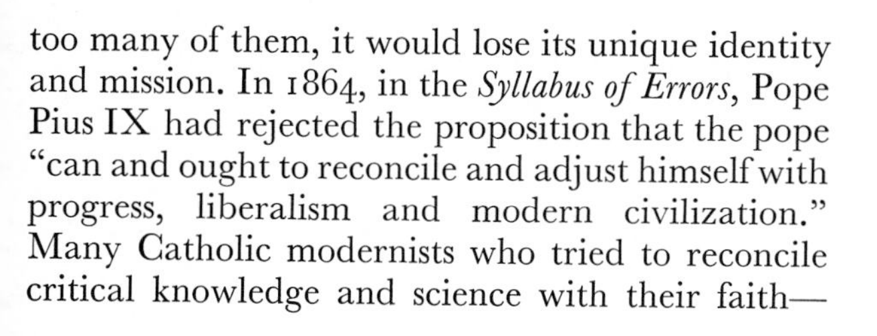

too many of them, it would lose its unique identity and mission. In 1864, in the *Syllabus of Errors*, Pope Pius IX had rejected the proposition that the pope "can and ought to reconcile and adjust himself with progress, liberalism and modern civilization." Many Catholic modernists who tried to reconcile critical knowledge and science with their faith—notably Father George Tyrrell (1861–1909) in England and Alfred Loisy (1857–1940) in France—were sincere in their faith but found their defense of Catholicism rejected. Loisy—who argued that, since the Church was the continuation of what the Bible began, revelation was not confined to scriptures—was excommunicated in 1908.

The Situation Today

Christian churches in the middle of the 20th century share two common concerns: increasing social responsibility and broad religious apathy. Theologians grappling with the second of these problems have not agreed on an answer, partly because contemporary philosophy is unsympathetic to their speculation, and partly because so many formulations have been tried and found wanting. In our own time, some Protestant churchmen have declared that God (as Christianity has known him) is dead; and the German theologian Paul Tillich (1886–1965) suggests that he represents "man's ultimate concern." Groups practicing Christian ethics have won followings without relating practice to dogma.

The problem of whether it is possible to separate the content of Christianity from its form is expressed by Rudolph Bultmann (born 1884). He argues that since the form of Christianity was originally meant only for the people it first reached, Jews with a messianic tradition and Hellenistically-oriented peoples of the first century, the message of the Gospel must now find a form for modern men. The opposite point of view can be found in the writings of the Swiss theologian Karl Barth (1886–1968), who saw salvation not in men, who have so clearly failed, but in unconditional faith in Christ as a bridge between God and man.

Protestant and Catholic churches have turned their attention increasingly to social problems. Priests in France and Italy have left their churches to work in factories and take Christianity to those who have rejected or forgotten it. In France and Germany, Christian Socialist parties are active in politics. In South America priests and monks are promoting better welfare and increased social justice for people who live in generally appalling conditions. Ministers in the United States are active in civil rights movements. In general the church is admitting responsibility for the quality of human life here on earth, in many cases irrespective of the possibility of converting the people they help.

Christianity has always attracted hostility, but it is only in our own time that large numbers of people have found it irrelevant. It is perhaps this apathy which has led Christians to try to overcome their differences. Pope John XXIII (1958–63) was in-

Above: Protestant church in Cutchogue, Long Island. Changing its attitude to the Protestant Reformation, the Roman Catholic Church now regards Protestants as "separated brethren," not heretics. Below: Dome of the Rock, a famous Moslem shrine, stands on a site sacred to Moslems, Christians and Jews in Jerusalem, a center of pilgrimage for all three religions. Although Christians are drawing closer together, political rivalries in the Middle East prevent these three faiths from reaching a better understanding.

Top: Pierre Teilhard de Chardin (1881–1955), French Jesuit and paleontologist. Ordained in 1912, he later developed a controversial theory of evolution reconciling science and religion. Above: Karl Barth, well-known Protestant theologian (1886-1968). A Swiss pastor, Barth set out to challenge liberal Protestantism in his famous commentary *The Epistle to the Romans*, first published in 1918. He believed that Christ was the link between God and man, and salvation could only be given through him.

Above: American evangelist Billy Graham at a prayer meeting. Conducting spiritual crusades all over the world, he has won many thousands of immediate converts by his dynamic preaching. Although some church leaders doubt the permanency of these quick conversions, many strongly support Graham.

strumental in encouraging a new, if tentative, spirit of tolerance and cooperation. Protestant churches are working together on an unprecedented scale for greater unity in the ecumenical movement.

The Catholic Church has survived largely by remaining apostolic and authoritative through centuries of hostility. Whether or not it will respond effectively to modern apathy may depend on making greater changes than it has ever made, faster than it has ever made them. Modernization until now has adjusted to the needs of the congregation—the Mass no longer has to be said in Latin. But growing numbers of priests are leaving the Church to marry and have a devout family life, and Rome's position on contraception alienates many good Catholics and is flouted by others.

Two other aspects of contemporary religion are more positive. In countries where the state has apparently succeeded in repressing religion, the Soviet Union for example, young people are beginning to find the notion of God satisfying. In western Europe and the United States, the contemplative side of Eastern religions like Hinduism and Buddhism is attracting inquirers and practitioners.

GREEK PHILOSOPHY

The key to the greatness of the Greeks was their curiosity. They wanted to understand the nature of the world for the sake of knowledge, rather than simply to be able to solve specific problems. By reasoning according to general principles, the Greeks brought a logical element to their speculations which had been lacking in the inquiries of earlier civilizations and which marks the beginning of philosophic and scientific thought.

Left: Plato, in this Pompeiian mosaic, is shown expounding an argument to the members of his school, the Academy. Named after its site, the grove of Academus outside Athens, it is believed to be the first of its kind in history—a school devoted solely to knowledge rather than vocational ends.

Early Greek Cosmologists

The story of philosophy begins at the town of Miletus, on the shores of the Aegean, to the east of present-day Greece. There, in the sixth century B.C., an Ionian Greek named Thales (about 640–546 B.C.) speculated about the origin and nature of the universe. In so doing, he became the world's first philosopher.

No one knows why philosophy began when and where it did, although it is interesting that it began not in the cities on the Greek mainland but in the colonies around the edges of the Greek world. Long before the time of Thales, man had laid the foundations of astronomy by watching the stars. But astronomy is only one subject. Thales' achievement was to ask a novel question about the world as a whole. He wanted to find a single basic substance or element from which everything is made. Thales thought this is water: Everything, including (possibly) the gods, is made from it. Early in the present century, the accepted opinion was that everything originates from hydrogen, which when combined with oxygen forms water. Thales probably noticed that although water normally exists in a liquid state, it can also exist as a solid and as a gas. This may have given him the idea that its liquid form is the underlying substance from which everything else is made. He also thought that the earth floated in water.

Anaximander (about 611–547 B.C.), an associate of Thales, thought that the primary substance is a boundless, indefinite Something, taking as many different forms as the things we see. He believed that the earth is a cylinder with a flat top and bottom which people walk on. This is probably the earliest theory that there is no true up and down.

Anaximenes (about 590–525 B.C.), the third of the Milesian nature-philosophers, also sought to discover the basic element from which everything else

The geography of Greece—isolated valleys and harbors, and scattered islands like this one, Delos—helped to keep communities separate from each other. This favored the creation of widely different schools of thought which could flourish close to each other and yet develop individually within their own geographical locale without influencing, rivaling or destroying each other's aims and efforts.

is made. He decided that it is air, which takes solid or liquid form when condensed and gaseous form when rarefied.

Meanwhile, about the time of Anaximenes, but to the north of Miletus, at Ephesus, Heraclitus (about 540–470 B.C.) was instructing people that at the heart of things there burns an everlasting, all-consuming fire. From this fire everything is begotten, to it everything will return. Heraclitus sometimes seems to have identified this fire with the Logos, or universal Reason as the law of change. However that may be, the speed of movement of physical fire gave Heraclitus the bridge he needed to the second part of his philosophy, which was that everything is in a state of perpetual change or flux. A man cannot step into the same river twice, he says, for it is not the same water both times. The third part of Heraclitus' philosophy was his belief that the change which is at the heart of things is always expressing itself in a strife between opposites which, coming together, produce kinds of unity which then dissolve again. This is like Hegel's theory (p. 136).

The early theories of the universe are in a sense scientific as well as philosophic since they are hypotheses about the natural world. But these early thinkers had little or no conception of inductive methods of experiment and verification as they are used in science today. Their search for a single substance probably sprang from a wish to find an underlying unity in life itself, which is one of the deepest desires of the human spirit. Moreover, the concepts in terms of which they thought were not the same as ours. Indeed, part of what makes the thought of any earlier epoch so hard to understand is the subtle change that occurs in the meanings of concepts throughout the centuries. Finally, and perhaps most important, our knowledge about all philosophers before Plato comes to us only from stories told about them and from later philosophers such as Aristotle.

Thales (above left), the world's first philosopher, believed the earth is composed of water, which he probably knew exists in liquid, solid and gaseous forms. Anaximander (center) thought that the earth floats on water in the middle of the universe, the whole being supported by air. Heraclitus (right) taught that the center of the universe is fire, from which all things sprlng, including the state of perpetual change obvious in both physical and spiritual worlds. The essence of life, he believed, is struggle.

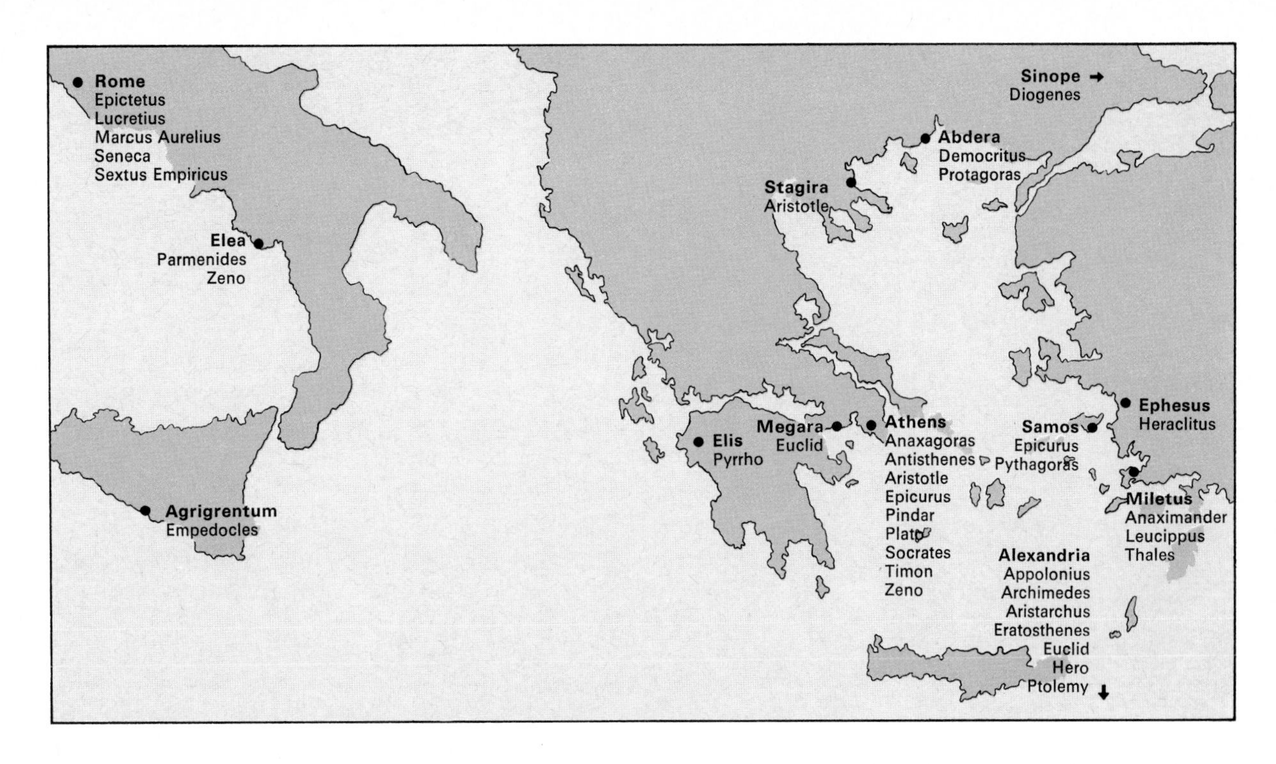

Above: this map shows the places where the Greek philosphers lived and taught. Our Western civilization is based on the philosophic and scientific tradition that grew up in ancient Greece and which began two and a half thousand years ago in Miletus, a busy Ionian trading town. Curiosity and inquiry about the nature of the world probably arose because of the town's commercial contact with other nations.

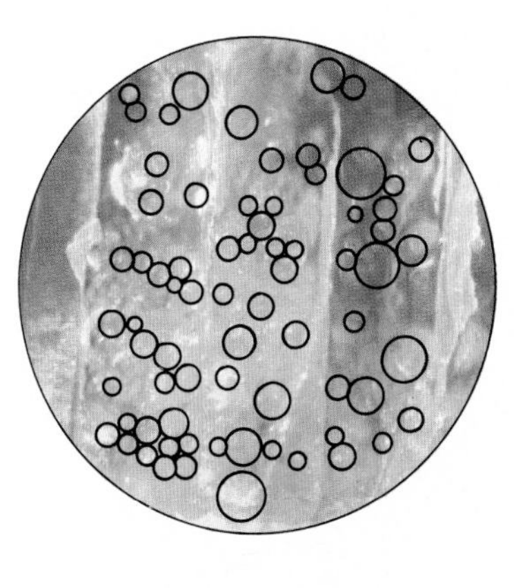

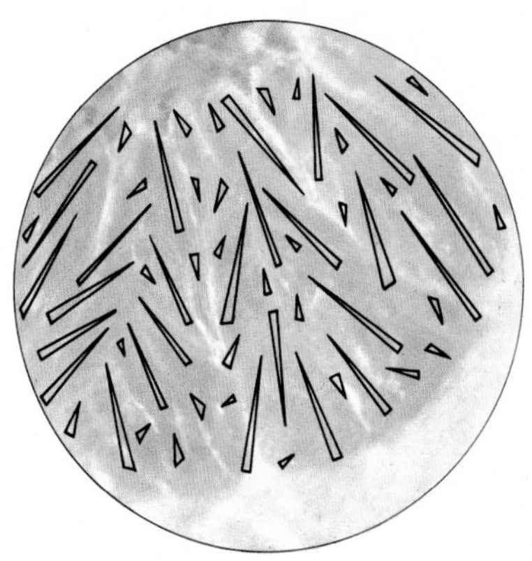

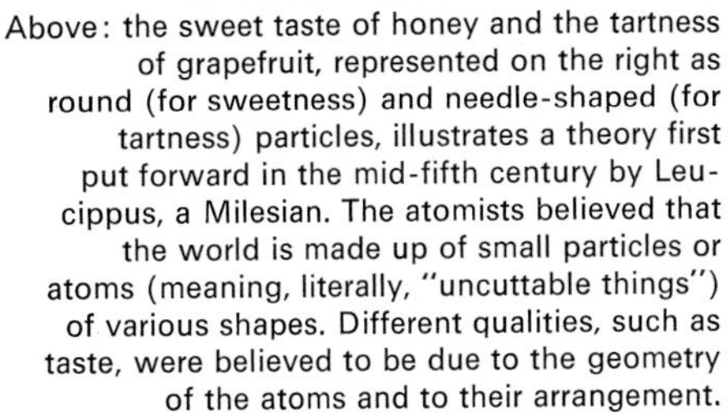

Above: the sweet taste of honey and the tartness of grapefruit, represented on the right as round (for sweetness) and needle-shaped (for tartness) particles, illustrates a theory first put forward in the mid-fifth century by Leucippus, a Milesian. The atomists believed that the world is made up of small particles or atoms (meaning, literally, "uncuttable things") of various shapes. Different qualities, such as taste, were believed to be due to the geometry of the atoms and to their arrangement.

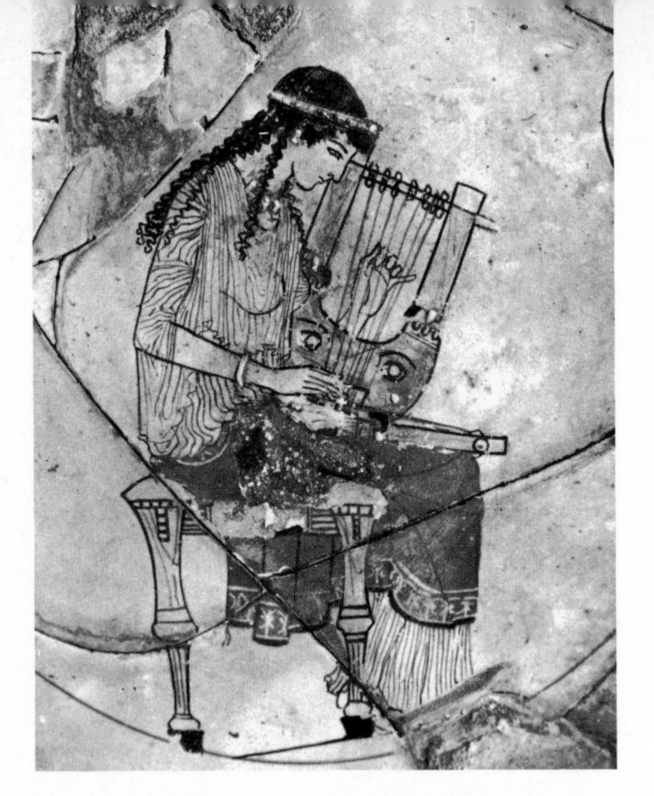

Above: girl playing a cithara. The Pythagoreans discovered the relationship between string lengths and musical harmony.

Below: Euclid of Alexandria, whose *The Elements of Geometry* determined the way geometry was taught for nearly 2,000 years.

Pythagoras

A very different school of thought developed at the same time as the Milesian tradition. This was the school of Pythagoras which flourished in Italy during the sixth century B.C.

Pythagoras (about 582–500 B.C.) was a mathematician of genius who was also a mystic. He thought that the whole universe is based on numbers. The theorem for which he is remembered in geometry is that in a right-angled triangle the sum of the squares of the sides next to the right angle equals the square of the third side, or hypotenuse.

The Pythagoreans also studied mathematical relationships between sounds. For example, strings which differ in length produce notes of different pitch. What Pythagoras and the secret brotherhoods which he founded discovered was that when two such notes are sounded together, they make a pleasant sound only if their lengths stand in specific numerical relationships to each other, such as three to two (a musical fifth) or two to one (an octave). Modern science accepts this, but dismisses another Pythagorean belief that the distances between planets correspond to the numerical intervals in the musical scale. The Pythagoreans thought that the planets revolve around a central fire (not, apparently, the sun), producing as they travel heavenly sounds called the music of the spheres.

Pythagoras thought that numbers possess certain nonmathematical properties such as character, shape, dimension and even sex. Five was the number of marriage because it was a combination of the first even or female number, two, and the first male or odd number, three. Generally, even numbers were considered bad, and odd numbers good. The number one was the godhead or source from which all numbers sprang. The Pythagoreans also believed that a line is made up of a definite number of units. They would not have understood the notion of infinite divisibility and were disturbed when they found that it was impossible to discover the square root of two.

The occult side of Pythagoras' teachings was probably inspired by the mystery religions of ancient Greece. Before the philosophers struck out in new directions, there had been two major currents in Greek thought. The Homeric tradition urged men to live like heroes and to think as little as possible about the unpleasant, ghost-like conditions of life

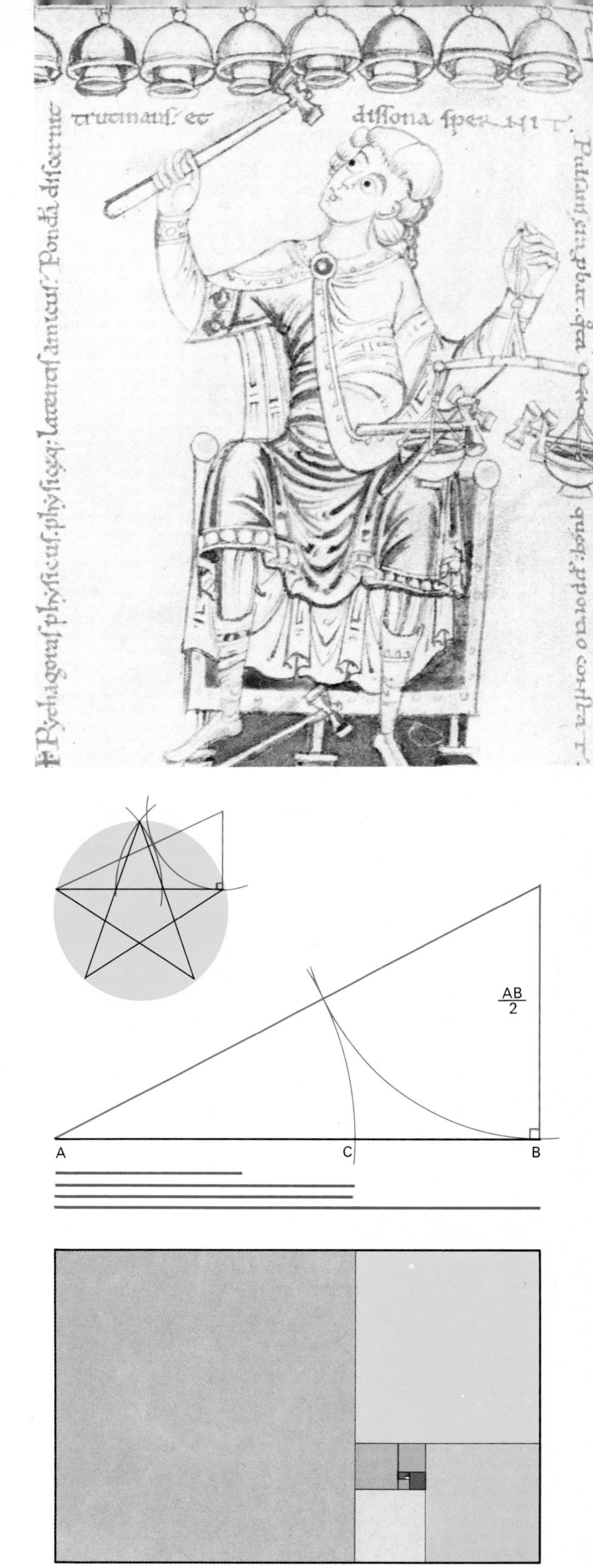

Right: Pythagoras is shown tuning bells in this 13th-century illustration from *De Musica* by Boethius. Pythagoras believed that without harmony and balance nothing could be perfect.

after death. The mystery religions, whose teachings Pythagoras followed, claimed that there was nothing alarming about the next world, and that man could be initiated into its wonderful secrets while still on earth. Mathematical understanding was itself part of this initiation. The belief of these ancient religions in a world of spirit passed from Pythagoras through Plato into the mainstream of European thought, where it fused with Christianity to form the basis of the spiritual outlook which exists today.

Very little is known about Pythagoras himself. He was born on the Greek island of Samos and is said to have studied in Egypt and Persia before founding a colony in the Greek city of Croton in southern Italy. He left no writings, and for many years his followers attributed their own discoveries to him, so we cannot know his real beliefs.

Right: the "golden section," used by the Pythagoreans to construct their symbol, the regular pentagram; the line AB is divided at C so that CB is to AC as AC is to AB. The section involves an irrational number, an upsetting discovery as it refuted the theory that any line is made up of an exact number of whole units.
Below: Pythagoras' theorem: the square of the hypotenuse of a right-angled triangle equals the sum of the squares of the other sides.

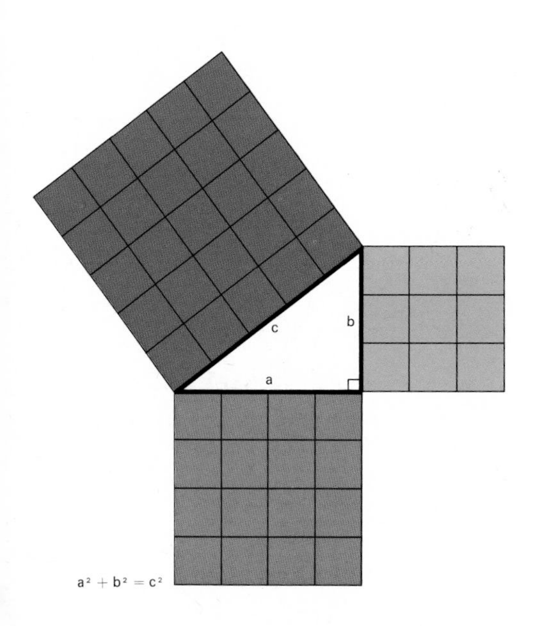

From the One to the Many

This illuminated manuscript shows Plato sitting at his desk. In the works of Plato, the main schools of Greek philosophy before Socrates were combined. His theory of knowledge relies on the merging of ideas from both Parmenides and Heraclitus. In mathematics Plato, like Zeno, denied the Pythagoreans, unit theory.

The reaction against the Milesian world-view with which philosophy began was initiated by Parmenides (about 515–440 B.C.), from Elea in southern Italy. Although he agreed with the Milesians that there is only one substance, he denied that the parts of the substance can move about, something which had hitherto been taken for granted. Parmenides, in other words, denied the reality of change. One reason given by Parmenides for thinking that change is an illusion was that if there is only one substance, its parts must form an indivisible whole. In that case, he thought, there can be nowhere for them to move.

Zeno (about 490–430 B.C.), a pupil of Parmenides, tried to prove the impossibility of motion by a number of paradoxes. The most famous concerns a race between Achilles and a tortoise. Achilles, a fair-minded man, gives the tortoise a head start. But he cannot win, or even catch the tortoise. By the time Achilles has reached the place where the tortoise was when the race started, the tortoise will have moved a little bit further on.

Suppose the race continues but is considered as if it had begun from these fresh starting points. The same thing will happen all over again. The distance between Achilles and the tortoise gets less all the time, but can never become zero. Each time Achilles reaches the place where the tortoise was a moment ago, he finds that the tortoise has used the time he took to reach it to move further on. Of course, we know that in such a race Achilles would catch and pass the tortoise, but Zeno's point was that our perception of such motion must be illusory, since in reason and therefore in reality it is impossible.

Although no one could find what was wrong with

Left: a coin showing Anaxagoras (about 500–428 B.C.), an Ionian living in Athens who believed all matter to be a mixture of opposites. Its final appearance was due to the greater preponderance of one or another of the opposites. Right: Anaxagoras believed that even white skin contains some blackness. An enlarged photograph of the white hand (far right) seems to support his theory by showing black between the highlights.

Left: Democritus (about 420 B.C.), developing Leucippus' atomist theory, said that the world is made up of innumerable atoms in motion, although we see or feel it in various ways. The different combinations of atoms produce changes. Right: Democritus' theory expressed pictorially. In the first picture the black and white dots are mixed; in the second, all the black and all the white are grouped together, forming a hand.

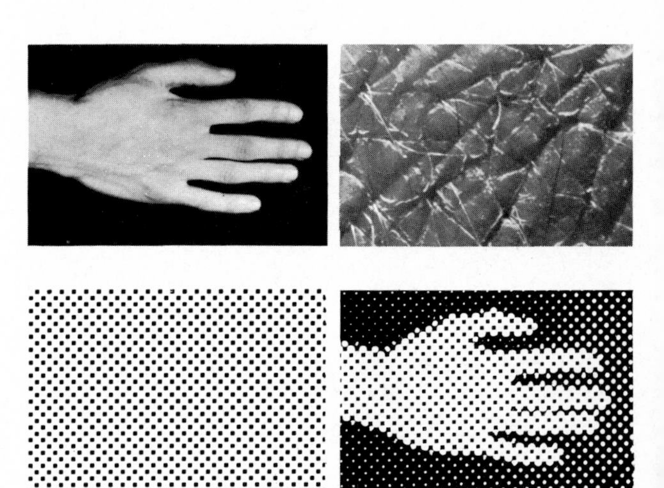

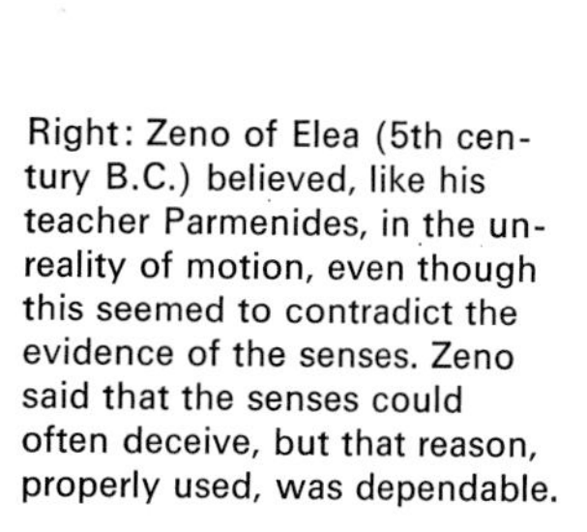

Right: Zeno of Elea (5th century B.C.) believed, like his teacher Parmenides, in the unreality of motion, even though this seemed to contradict the evidence of the senses. Zeno said that the senses could often deceive, but that reason, properly used, was dependable.

Zeno's paradoxes, the pendulum of thought soon swung to the other extreme. Instead of the single, frozen world-structures of Parmendides and Zeno, there was a reversion to the idea that the world is full of movement and life. Not that this idea had ever completely died out. The Sicilian Empedocles (about 490–430 B.C.), for example, who was a contemporary of Parmenides, believed that there are four distinct elements—earth, air, fire and water. The Ionian Anaxagoras (about 500–428 B.C.) believed that everything is infinitely divisible and that everything contains a portion of everything else. Anaxagoras also believed that the sun is a stone about the size of the Peloponnesus.

The philosophers who were reacting more specifically against Parmenides included the Milesian Leucippus (mid fifth century B.C.). Some scholars question whether in fact Leucippus ever lived, but if he did he was the founder of the *atomist* system of thought. Much more is known about the Thracian atomist Democritus (about 460–370 B.C.). Democritus believed that the universe consists of an infinite number of atoms which are always in motion and which cannot be divided or destroyed. Different qualities in the universe are caused by changing arrangements of the atoms.

As these various theories came and went, two other tendencies were also at work deep within the fabric of Greek thought. The Skeptics believed that real knowledge is impossible because reason leads to ludicrous conclusions and the senses can deceive. The first Skeptics were the Greek Pyrrho (about 365–275 B.C.) and his followers.

The Cynics rejected social conventions (they were called "Cynics" by others because they lived "like dogs") and were more interested in the virtues of living simply than in theories about the world. One of the founders of the school was Diogenes (about 412–323 B.C.), who is reported to have slept in a tub. There is a story that he was called on by Alexander the Great, who asked if he desired any favor. "Only to stand out of my light," replied Diogenes.

Above: Diogenes, the son of a moneychanger, born in Sinope, a Greek colony on the Euxine, got the nickname "Cynic" (meaning dog-like) because of the primitive way in which he lived—legend has it he lived in a tub. His aim was to acquire wisdom through life, not learning. He was thus not a cynic in the modern sense.

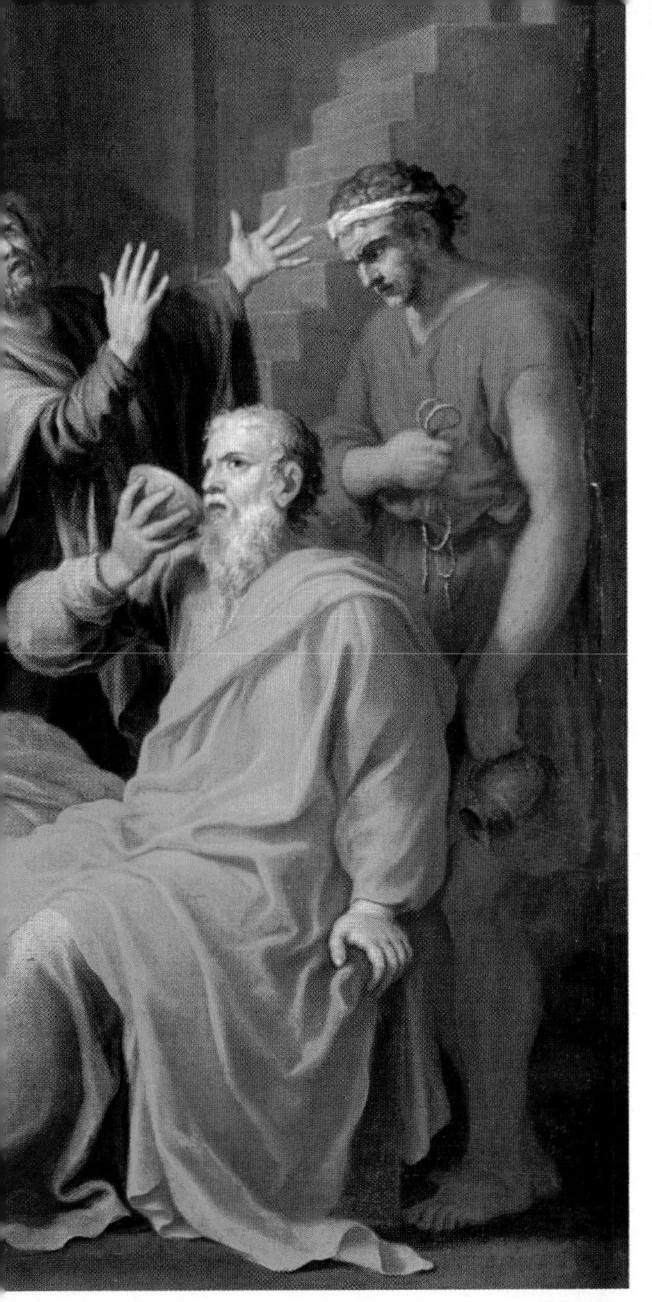

Socrates and the Sophists

Socrates (about 470–399 B.C.) did not write any philosophic works, but we know a great deal about him from Plato. He taught by speaking, very simply but with a force of logic that was indisputable. Reputedly very ugly, with a snub nose, Socrates would walk through the streets of Athens until he met someone he could draw into a discussion. The subject might be the nature of courage, the ideal society, or whether virtue could be taught. Whatever it was, Socrates would confess himself ignorant and unable to supply answers to the problem posed. In these discussions, described in Plato's dialogues, Socrates represents himself as a humble seeker after truth who is wiser than other men only because he realizes how little he knows. Perhaps the young friend he has fallen in with will be able to help him by answering a few simple questions. The friend answers confidently at first, then less so, as one by one his most cherished assumptions and ideas are exposed as false or misleading. Eventually it turns out that neither Socrates nor his companion can find the answers they seek. Inconclusive as such dialogues are, it is clear that Socrates is attempting to separate opinion, which is often false and contradictory, from knowledge, which is to be reached by deliberate and unprejudiced thought. It was in the course of these discussions that Socrates came up against the Sophists, a body of professional teachers of rhetoric and politics who preached that the proper study for man was neither the gods nor the scientific study of nature, but man himself. For them "man is the measure of all things." The Sophists claimed to be able to teach (for a suitable fee) young men of good family all they needed to know about philosophy, the art of living and public speaking. The Greek vase (below) shows such masters and pupils in an Athenian school. Socrates challenged their claims and discredited them. His conversation with Protagoras, their leader, is recounted in Plato's dialogue of that name. It is when Socrates delves into the nature of virtue and good citizenship, the very values that the Sophists claimed to teach, that Protagoras is lost. Socrates shows that these things cannot be defined with certainty, that there is no easy answer which can be taught, no real solution to the question. Socrates' inquiries into the nature of courage, justice or virtue offended not merely the Sophists but many other Athenians who disliked having their beliefs challenged. He was accused by a fellow citizen and brought to trial for corrupting young people and for impiety. When he refused to plead for mercy he was sentenced to death by poison. The painting on the left shows the death of Socrates, which Plato describes in his dialogue, *Phaedo*. Surrounded by friends, Socrates drinks the hemlock poison with the utmost serenity. Before he dies he gives a series of proofs of the immortality of the soul. His last words were to remind one friend of a debt he owed to another.

Plato, the Greek philosopher. His real name was Aristocles, but he was given the nickname Plato, which means "broad-shouldered." Born about 427 B.C., he was statesman and poet as well as thinker. In his *Dialogues* he immortalizes the ideas of his teacher, Socrates.

One of the greatest philosophers of all times was Plato (427–347 B.C.). His views have remained influential throughout history and his ideas and ideals form part of man's Western heritage.

Plato was an Athenian of noble family, who as a young man was very much influenced by Socrates. Later he founded the Academy, so named because it was located in the grove of Academus, outside Athens. It survived for nine centuries and was a forerunner of the modern university.

Central to Plato's philosophy was the belief that there is a world of timeless, changeless ideas or archetypes, sometimes called "forms," of which the world of ordinary experience is an imperfect imitation. With this theory Plato becomes the most powerful advocate of the belief, central to religions the world over, that the world man experiences through the senses is not the only one there is. According to Plato, it mirrors a world of eternal ideas which can only ever be known by the mind.

The higher world is linked to the world of everyday life by the qualities which different things have in common. For example, roses, buttercups and daffodils all share the form of a flower. Similarly, beautiful objects share the form of beauty. While objects are perceived only by the senses, Plato thought that with reflection the mind should be able to perceive the idea or pure form of beauty which the objects have in common.

Plato no doubt hoped that this theory would lead people towards mystical experience through rational thought. But unfortunately, if his arguments were valid, he proved too much. For as Plato himself later admitted, the same arguments which proved the existence of the good, the beautiful and the true would also prove the existence of forms that were less desirable. Ugly and unimportant things would need forms as well.

Another belief close to Plato's heart was that the soul is immortal. In his dialogue called the *Phaedrus*, the soul is compared to a winged creature whose normal abode is the celestial regions, where it travels through the heavens in a chariot in the company of the gods. One of the chariot's horses is spirit and the other is desire, and the two pull in different directions until the chariot is overturned. The soul becomes giddy and spirals earthwards, losing its wings. When it regains consciousness it

Above: an Attic bell-krater, which illustrates Plato's *Phaedrus* myth. The white horse, symbolizing the soul, is in conflict with the red horses, representing desire. Because they pull in different directions, the chariot overturns and falls to earth.

Right: a page from one of the earliest manuscripts of Plato's works, as copied in A.D. 895. This page shows the end of the *Protagoras* and the beginning of the *Gorgias*. Of all the classical philosophers, Plato is the only one whose works have come down to us nearly complete (Bodleian MS. E.D. Clarke 39, f.368v).

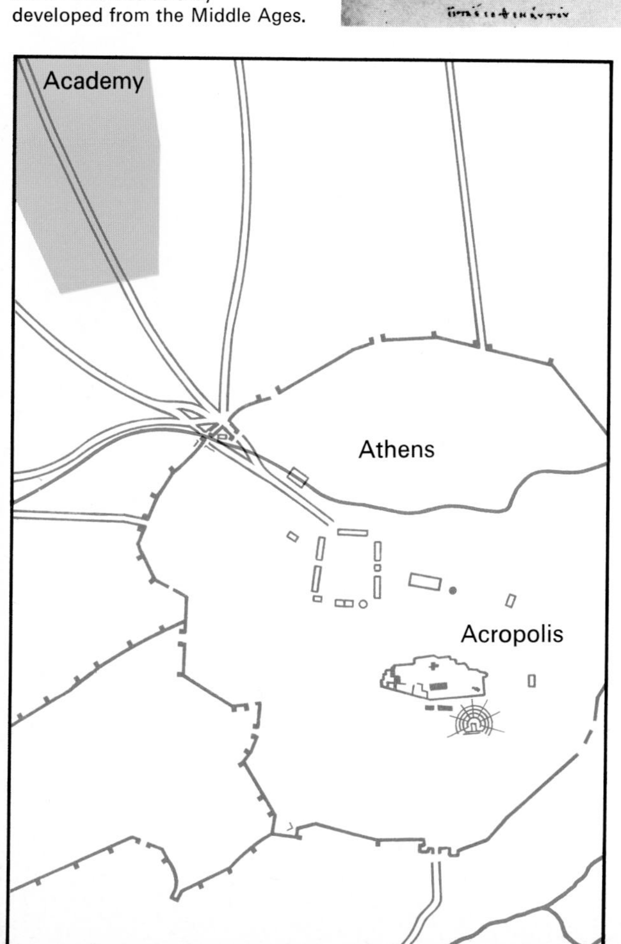

Below: the site of Plato's school, the Academy, a mile from Athens. The foundations were laid in 387 B.C. and it survived for over nine hundred years—longer than any such institution before or since. The Academy is the ancestor of the universities as they developed from the Middle Ages.

is imprisoned in a body and has lost its memory.

Plato supported the belief that the soul existed before the body arguing that all learning is a matter of recollecting what we once knew before. He tried to show how this might be possible by making Socrates question a slave boy about the properties of a square. When the boy has been led so far, he gives the right answer. But how can he do this, unless in some sense he knew it before? The argument is a subtle one. An analogy that might help is the case where the playing of a forgotten tune revives the memory of it. Unless the tune were already known, it could not be recognized.

In addition to other dialogues of incomparable prose covering a whole range of philosophic problems Plato wrote the *Republic*, possibly the greatest work on political philosophy ever written. The solution recommended for the problems of society was to put the affairs of the city-state in the hands of philosopher-kings, who could apply their knowledge of the world of pure forms to the problems of human life. Plato thought that the perfect state was unlikely to be realized on earth but he believed it was a goal to be worked toward.

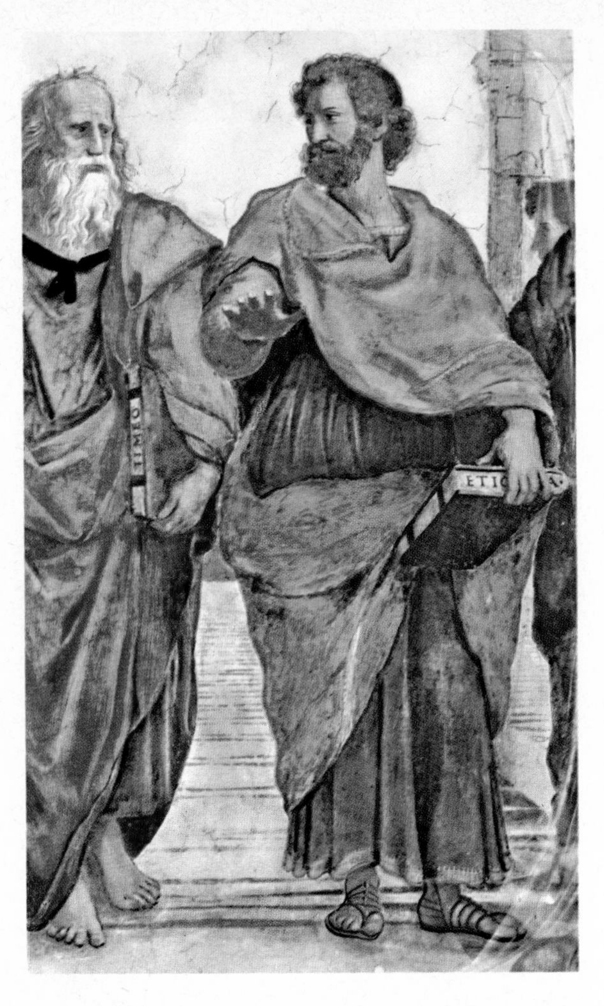

Above: Plato and Aristotle, a detail from Raphael's *The School of Athens*. Aristotle went to study at Plato's Academy at the age of 17 and remained there for 20 years. While Plato emphasized metaphysics, and studied the nature of reality as a whole, Aristotle was active in virtually every field of study known at the time.

THE TEN ARISTOTELIAN CATEGORIES	
Substance	Andrew Witherspoon
Quality	Admiral
Quantity	Six foot + two inches
Relation	Fleet Commander
Place	Lat. 45° N Long. 30° W
Time	14.00 G.M.T.
Position	Standing on the deck
State	Wet
Action	Shouting into megaphone
Affection	Being buffeted by storm

Aristotle

Aristotle (384–322 B.C.) was the most famous pupil at Plato's Academy. He went to Athens from Thrace in 366, leaving only after Plato died. Plato was mainly influential in metaphysics, which tries to discover the meaning of existence and the purpose of life. Aristotle lectured and wrote on many subjects, including physics, astronomy and especially biology. In philosophy his influence has been very great in ethics and political theory as well as in metaphysics; but he has been most influential in logic, which studies the general conditions of valid reasoning.

Aristotle's great discovery was the syllogism, an argument consisting of three parts: a major premise, a minor premise and a conclusion. There are various kinds of syllogism, but the best known example is, "All men are mortal, Socrates is a man, therefore Socrates is mortal." This is an argument from the general to the particular, in that it begins with a class, cites an instance of it, and then comes to a conclusion about the instance. Such arguments are called deductive.

There are also arguments called inductive, which reason from the particular to the general. An example is, "The sun has always risen in the past, so will rise tomorrow." The claim here is that the large number of occasions on which the sun has risen in the past makes it reasonable to suppose that it will rise tomorrow. It might be thought that this is an argument from the general to the particular, like the argument about Socrates. But that would be a mistake. The major premise in the argument about Socrates contains all the members of the class of men. The major premise in the argument about the sun, however, contains only some of the mem-

Left: In his ten categories Aristotle defines the functions of language. The first is substance, which is *what* we talk about (in this case an admiral); the other categories show, in general, *how* we talk about it. Language is thus not haphazard—it is used by men to cope with the world about them. It reflects reality.

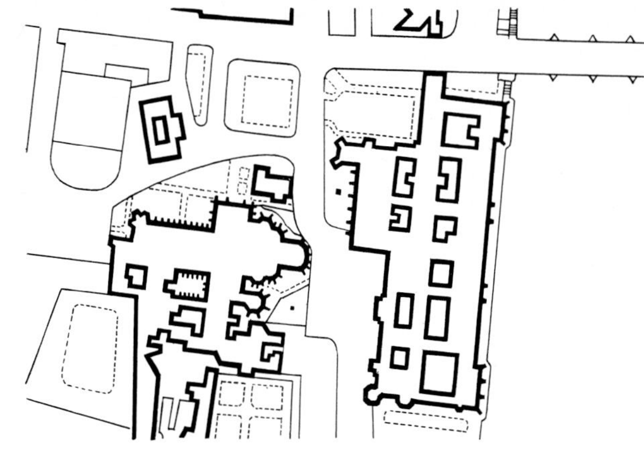

Above left: an aerial photograph of Westminster, London, alongside a plan of exactly the same area. The usefulness of a plan depends on the accuracy of its correspondence to the subject it represents. For Aristotle, language is a "plan" or "map" reflecting reality. If we are to distinguish various types of statements and argue correctly, our concepts must correspond to reality, and our judgments are true when our concepts are linked in the way that the physical features of an area are linked in a map or plan.

bers of the class of sunrises; namely, those which will have occurred before tomorrow morning. Admittedly, the conclusion is in terms of a particular day, tomorrow. But that is a false lead. The full conclusion to be drawn from the argument is that the sun will continue to rise unless the laws of nature change; provided, of course, that nothing happens to stop it rising from within those laws.

Aristotle made extensive studies of the habits and structure of animals, and his principles for thinking correctly in argument and in scientific inquiry also led him to rules for classification by genus and species which still survive in biology. His study of deductive reasoning has been the basis of logic ever since, although it has only recently been greatly expanded in modern symbolic logic.

In philosophy, Aristotle's most important theory concerned evolution, which he took in its widest sense to mean the development of anything towards an end or goal. He thought that the final stage of development is already contained in the first stage in latent form. The hen, for example, exists potentially in the egg, the flower in the seed. So things in the process of changing can be understood only in terms of their potentialities. The actuality toward which a thing changes, which determines its development, Aristotle also called its "form." He regarded the form as "immanent," existing within the object. So Aristotle's theory of forms must be distinguished from Plato's, whose forms were "transcendent"; they existed outside their objects, and independently of them.

The final form of all, for Aristotle, is God. He regarded God as form without matter. God draws the evolving universe towards him by the very fact that he exists, but he himself is beyond all striving, beyond all change. He does not even pay any attention to the universe. Indifferent to its progress, remote from all human affairs, he contemplates his own existence throughout eternity.

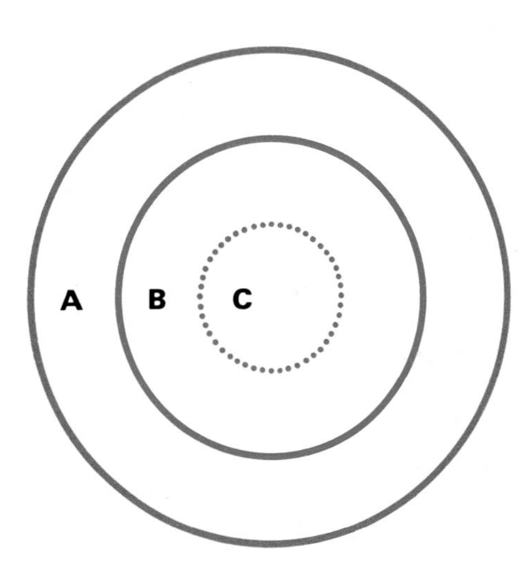

A diagrammatic method of testing syllogistic arguments, invented by the 18th-century Swiss mathematician, Leonhard Euler. (Above) all B are A, all C are B, therefore all C are A. (Below) no B are A, all C are B, therefore no C are A.

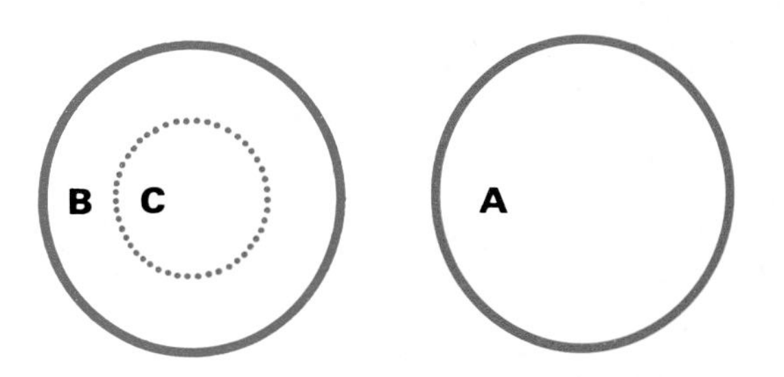

Stoics and Epicureans

By about 300 B.C., the great days of Greece were over. The Greek genius continued to flower fitfully for some centuries, but the fire which originally imbued it never returned. Meanwhile, with the departure of giants like Plato and Aristotle, the great playwrights and poets, and above all the Greek city-states with their built-in systems of morality and religion, the average Greek was left without any clear idea of how he ought to live. The Stoic and Epicurean systems arose to meet his need.

These systems were far more concerned with

Above: Chrysippus (277–206 B.C.) greatly increased the influence of the Stoics by reorganizing them and systematizing their beliefs. He taught that good and evil always went together, but that God, in whose existence he believed, was not responsible for evil.
Below: an olive grove in Greece. The traditional Greek belief in many gods contrasts with Stoicism, which taught a form of pantheism (the belief that the natural world is a manifestation of God).

A reconstruction of the Stoa of Attalus, first built in the second century B.C. The new building, now the Agora Museum, stands in the Street of the Panathenaia, Athens, on the site of its original. A feature is a colonnade of 45 columns with Doric bases and Ionic tops.

morality then with philosophy as such. It is true that Epicurus (about 342–270 B.C.), founder of the Epicureans, adopted the atomist theory of Democritus (p. 89). Zeno of Citium (about 340–265 B.C.), who founded Stoicism, also believed firmly that the universe is governed by unbreakable laws. (Zeno's views were sometimes obscure, however. He is reported to have said that God runs through the world like honey through a honeycomb.) But the real problem which concerned both these schools was how men should live.

Stoics and Epicureans shared a belief in the worth of man as an individual. This in itself was a revolutionary notion compared with the view held in many of the old city-states. There man was regarded first as a citizen who owed duties to the state. His individuality was secondary.

If the Stoics and Epicureans agreed on the importance of man, they disagreed on practically everything else. The Stoics taught that nothing matters but virtue, while the Epicureans taught that nothing matters but happiness. Stoicism, by far the more important of the two schools historically, assumed that life is a dismal affair with which men must come to terms as best they can. The Stoic masters preached obedience to the law and universal love, but the key to their ethics was that man must remain emotionally detached. They believed there are certain events man can control. Other events cannot be controlled and should be accepted as the will of God. This aloofness and detachment, which they called "apathy," meaning, literally, the absence of emotion, led to curious results. There is a story that when the Stoic slave Epictetus was being tortured by his master, he remarked with composure, "If you go on like that, you will certainly break my leg." A few minutes later, the leg broke. "Did I not tell you that you would break it?" said Epictetus. Virtue, for the Stoics, consisted mainly of an iron selfcontrol.

The Epicurean outlook was very different from that of the Stoics. The gentle leader of this school taught his followers that the object of life is the pursuit of happiness and the avoidance of physical and mental pain. Tranquillity could most easily be found in the enjoyment of simple pleasures. Epicurus also tried to bring tranquillity and peace to people by removing their fears about the gods and about death. He taught that death is simply the dispersion of all the atoms that form the body. Epicurus advised people not to bother about the gods on the grounds that they were too remote to be concerned with the humdrum lives of humans.

Above: Epicurus, an anti-religionist who believed the aim of life was happiness. His doctrine was immortalised 200 years later by the Roman poet Lucretius in his poem *De rerum natura*.

Above: Plotinus, an intellectual mystic, whose highly interesting views were generally only expressed in very abstract form. One of his beliefs was that souls inhabiting human bodies in this life might pass into animal, bird, or even vegetable forms of existence if they misused their god-given faculties. Too speculative a philosopher might, for example, become an eagle in another life.

The Neoplatonists, as the name suggests, were a school of philosophers who drew their inspiration from Plato, but they emphasized the mystical rather than the logical side of the master's teaching. They believed that the universe consists of a hierarchy of worlds, or planes of being, depending for their existence on an indefinable principle called the One. From this source of all life, far beyond man's understanding, the succession of worlds streamed forth in descending order, each giving birth in turn to the world beneath it. Each world, or plane of being, therefore, although ultimately dependent on the One, derived its immediate existence from the world above it, in whose image it is fashioned and to which it always strives to return. There is thus an outgoing journey and a return, somewhat on the principle of a fountain. Mankind is supposed to be in the world which is furthest away from the original source, but still sharing more of the One than animals, plants and inanimate objects.

By far the most important Neoplatonist was the Egyptian Plotinus (about 205–270), one of the greatest mystics of all time. His teacher was a mysterious man called Ammonius Saccas (175–242), who seems to have stood in much the same relation to Plotinus as Socrates did to Plato. Plotinus studied under Saccas in Alexandria for 11 years,

between the ages of 28 and 39. He then attached himself to the army of the Roman emperor, who happened to be marching into Persia, in the hope that he might manage to acquire some of the lost wisdom of the East. The expedition came to an abrupt end, however, and after various adventures Plotinus turned up in Rome. He settled down comfortably and later became famous as a lecturer. His major work is the *Enneads*, a collection of 54 lectures and articles assembled by his disciple and biographer Porphyry (about 233–304). Porphyry arranged them in six books of nine essays each. Unfortunately, however, although Plotinus himself was a most interesting man, given to all sorts of psychic experiences, the *Enneads* are for the most part very abstruse and difficult to understand.

Plotinus divided his universe into a trinity of the One, the *Nous* (Mind) and the *Psyche* (Soul). He made a fundamental distinction between the One and the other two members of the trinity, on the grounds that whereas both of those have being, of however rarefied a sort, the One is the *source* of being. The One is also inexpressible and quite beyond man's power to comprehend. "While it is nowhere," said Plotinus, "nowhere is it not." This is reminiscent of the *Tao Te Ching* (p. 35) of China. The same mysterious principle was recognized by the *Upanishads* of India (p. 26), which declared: "The mind falls back from it, unable to reach it." Plotinus called the principle the One or the Good for convenience, but he warned that such names were only labels which could easily mislead.

As the sun radiates light, the One gave rise to the Nous, which mirrors or reflects it. Nous is a difficult word to translate, but Universal Mind or Spirit perhaps come nearest the mark. The Nous in turn gave birth to the Psyche, or World Soul, which is the principle that pervades the material world of man. It is the World Soul that is responsible for nature, and for the sun, moon and stars. Unlike the Universal Mind, which is indivisible, the World Soul can either preserve its identity inside the Nous, or split up and unite with the individual souls of men.

An individual human being, for Plotinus, is a spark of the eternal One imprisoned in a material body, and its salvation is to be reunited with the One. But this requires the most severe kinds of moral and intellectual discipline, and Plotinus claimed to have achieved it himself only for a few brief moments.

Neoplatonism had a profound influence on Christianity, especially through St. Augustine (p. 104) two centuries later.

Left: a third-century mural from Dura Europos in Mesopotamia showing Ezekiel's vision of the valley of the dry bones. Philo (50–20 B.C.), a Neoplatonist, believed, as did the Jews, that an infinite God could communicate with his finite creatures through intermediary "powers." These were not very different from the biblical angels shown here, who were God's recognized instruments in revitalizing the dead.

EARLY CHRISTIAN AND MEDIEVAL PHILOSOPHY

During the first centuries after the death of Christ, philosophy became essentially the servant of theology. Early Christian thinkers attempted to defend their faith and yet show that Greek philosophy did not stand in opposition to Christianity. In attempting to determine the relationship of faith and reason, opinion ranged from the belief that faith is necessary for reason to operate, to the view that faith and reason are wholly independent.

St. Augustine of Hippo has been called the first modern man because he combined insatiable curiosity with great learning. Interested in everything from astrology to witchcraft, his main preoccupation was theology. He tried to reconcile Biblical teaching with Greek philosophy.

Early Christian Philosophers

Let no one suppose the early Christian philosophers were meek and mild, after the manner of Christian saints in children's Bibles. At least in Egyptian Alexandria, they could not afford to be. This was a great cosmopolitan center where East and West met. In the centuries immediately succeeding Christ's death, mystics from the Orient rubbed shoulders with Greek philosophers, and many sects tried to penetrate and influence the new religion. Such a situation called for strong, tough, forthright characters among the Christians if their religion was not to lose its identity in the first few centuries of its existence. Luckily for Christianity, such men appeared. The intellectual defense of Christianity in pagan Alexandria was equaled only in the results achieved by the martyrdoms in Rome.

The first great Christian philosopher was Origen of Alexandria (about 185–254). He had been the brilliant though hot-tempered pupil of Ammonius Saccas (p. 98) and of Clement (p. 53), a literary scholar who was also a Christian Neoplatonist. Origen's teachings therefore had undertones of Neoplatonism and he was one of the first to link Christianity with the intellectual framework of Greek philosophy. Origen was the son of a martyr, and he thirsted for martyrdom too. He emasculated himself to get rid of the temptations which might divert him from his faith.

Among the religious sects which the fiery Origen combated was a semi-mystical sect of philosophers known as Gnostics. They believed the world had been created by a Demiurge or Fallen Spirit, because God would never have created such an evil place. This theory aroused the wrath not merely of Origen, but of Irenaeus and Tertullian (p. 53) in the West, and Clement in the East. The Gnostic view did not prevail, but Gnosticism left its mark on Christianity in other ways. For example, the

Left: an illustration from an Anglo-French biblical history of the 14th century, which shows the all-powerful Christian God, the supreme architect or geometer, creating the universe with a turn of his miraculous compasses.

Gnostic belief that there is a host of intermediaries between God and man had the effect of intensifying the Christian belief in saints and angels.

Some of Origen's views were condemned as heretical after his death. For one thing, he gave God the Father a more important position in the Trinity than the Son or Holy Ghost. This shows the extent to which the ideas of the early Christians were in a state of flux until church doctrines were agreed upon at the Council of Nicaea (A.D. 325). Strictly speaking, concepts like the Trinity belong to the domain of theology rather than philosophy, for the theologian starts from articles of faith which the philosopher calls into question.

Another early defender of the Church was Athanasius (about 296–373), who became Bishop of Alexandria just after the Council of Nicaea. He lacked Origen's erudition but made up for this by a strength of character which held the Church together for nearly 50 years, through all sorts of crises. Alexandria, under Athanasius, fully justified its claim to be the second city in Christendom.

What would it have felt like to have lived in these early times? During the first few centuries of the Christian era and in the ensuing twilight that men call the Dark Ages, a deep sense of gloom and a feeling of pessimism prevailed. Life was hard and too often sad. One reaction was to turn away from the visible world and to place hope in the unseen. Many Christians turned their eyes to the heavens and mortified the flesh. For a time, even learning was frowned upon. Whereas the early Christians had been earnest scholars, there is a letter from Pope Gregory the Great (590–604) to one of his bishops saying that the pope was shocked beyond measure to hear the bishop had been studying grammar. "A report has reached us which we cannot mention without a blush, that thou expoundest grammar to certain friends." There was at the same time during these centuries a yearning for personal experience and a personal God that found one of its first expressions in St. Augustine.

Above: a Gnostic cast showing one of their seven inferior creator-deities or Demiurges. Right: Christian believers in imperial Rome awaiting their martyrdom, perhaps by wild beasts in the public arenas.

Above: Origen, a fiery scholar who believed that the account of the Creation in Genesis answered all cosmological questions. It is said that he produced 6,000 rolls of manuscript, including commentaries on every book in the Old and New Testaments. He died at Tyre in 254 as a result of ill-treatment ordered by the Emperor Decius.

Left: the half-crazed Emperor Nero, during whose reign the persecution of Christians began. He believed they caused the fire that destroyed Rome in A.D. 64—and had many of them cruelly put to death.

St. Augustine

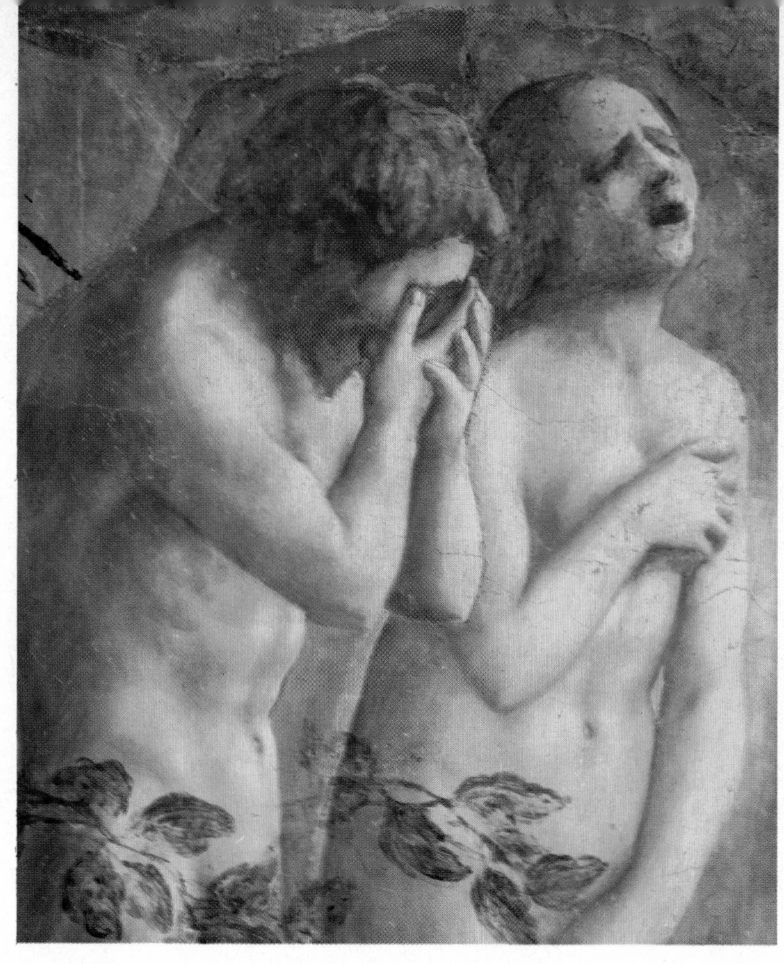

Right: this detail from a painting by Masaccio shows the expulsion of Adam and Eve from the Garden of Eden. By abusing God's gift of free will, they committed the original sin.

The wild and passionate nature of St. Augustine's youth is nowhere better recorded than in his own *Confessions*, the first, and perhaps the most famous, autobiography ever written. Augustine (354–430) was born in North Africa and when he was 16 went to live in Carthage. There he soon acquired a mistress, by whom he had a son. Gradually, however, a feeling of guilt began to intrude, which later developed into an overriding sense of sin. "What then did wretched I so love in thee, thou theft of mine, thou deed of darkness, in that sixteenth year of my age?" *(Confessions*, Book Two). Is Augustine perhaps talking about some early escapade with a girl? No, only about the theft of some pears from a neighbor's garden. He did not even eat them, but reflection on the incident continued to distress him for at least 20 years.

Oddly enough, it was also in a garden, some 15 years later, that Augustine had an experience which is said to have brought peace to his troubled soul. He had left Africa to become a lecturer in Milan, Italy, his mother having persuaded him to give up his mistress in favor of a bride-to-be. One day when Augustine was studying in a garden with a pupil, he was suddenly overcome with emotion. Making an excuse to his pupil, he flung himself down some way off in the garden to weep. While he was thus engaged, he heard a child's voice singing from over a wall. The story of this simple experience, and its effect, has become one of the great classics of the Christian religion. Shortly after the incident, Augustine was converted to Christianity by Ambrose (about 340–397) of Milan.

The deep sense of sin which plagued Augustine, at least until his conversion, is probably partly responsible for some of his more depressing beliefs. He believed that with the exception of a few people who are saved purely by the grace of God, human beings are damned and destined to go to hell. This is not so much because they have sinned themselves as because they are descended from Adam and Eve, who committed the original sin by eating the apple in the Garden of Eden. The whole of humanity has inherited this couple's guilt.

Before Augustine was converted to Christianity, he was successively a Skeptic, a Neoplatonist and a member of a sect of religious philosophers known as Manicheans, who believed that good and evil are powers which exist independently of man. Man sins when the evil power of darkness takes possession of him. This theory clashed with the Christian belief in original sin, so after his conversion Augustine denounced the Manicheans as heretics.

Augustine's doctrine of predestination contrasts with the teaching of Pelagius, a Welsh contemporary of the saint. Pelagius denied the doctrine of original

Far left: the title page of a 12th-century English manuscript of Augustine's *City of God* shows Christ defending the heavenly city from Satan. As there were six days of Creation, so history was a six-stage struggle between the forces of good and evil (Bodleian MS. Laud Misc. 469, fol. 7).
Left: an 11th-century manuscript illustration of the Pentecost, the descent of the Holy Spirit on the Apostles. Augustine held that God bestows such gifts where he wills and neither merit nor good works alter God's will.

Below: Augustine, as the Bishop of Hippo, in North Africa, a post he held from A.D. 396 until his death in A.D. 430. Throughout his life Augustine was obsessed with sin, and his famous *Confessions* are a colorful account of his struggles between good and evil. His ideas shaped early Christian theology.

sin and held that men were always free to choose good rather than evil.

When he was about 42, Augustine was made Bishop of Hippo, a city on the North African coast, where he lived until he died. It was here that, in addition to his *Confessions*, he wrote *The City of God*, which contrasts the life of a heavenly community of saints with communities on earth. The effect of this book in the West was to increase the power of the Church in relation to the state, for it implied that the state must take its orders from the Church on religious matters. In the East, where Augustine's book was less influential, the Church remained subservient to the state.

Augustine, as a good Christian, believed that God created the world out of nothing. His view differed from the Greek belief that God created the world from already-existing material, much as a potter might impress some form on a lump of clay. Augustine's preoccupation with the Creation led naturally to consideration of the nature of time. "What is time?" he asks. "If no one asks me, I know; but if I wish to explain to him who asks, I know not." Eventually he decided that God, as an Infinite Being, must be outside time. Time and the world came into existence together. It is therefore meaningless to ask whether there was anything before the Creation because there was no "before."

Above: This stained-glass window in Chartres Cathedral shows the departure of Charlemagne with his knights and a bishop. Crowned "Roman Emperor of the West" by Pope Leo in A.D. 800, Charlemagne recognized the pope's spiritual supremacy and held it his duty to defend the Church and the pope, and to uphold the faith. Below: Boethius, the Platonist philosopher and Roman patrician, writing *Consolation of Philosophy* while awaiting death in prison.

The Dark Ages

The fall of the Roman Empire in the fifth century brought an end to the rule of law which, however precariously, had held civilization together during the preceding centuries. The ancient world had consisted of the group of countries encircling the Mediterranean, and most of this area had been under Roman rule. The Romans were a politically-minded people, tolerant of ideas unless they were considered dangerous to the state. When a Christian community suddenly appeared in their midst, they first persecuted its members on the grounds that their ideas constituted a grave danger and then, when that did no good, they officially embraced Christianity. Greek members of Roman society, were allowed to live as they liked. Greek philosophers in those days were mainly Stoics and Neoplatonists, neither of whose ideas threatened the existence of the emperor-god at Rome.

Such was the situation at the beginning of the fifth century. But the Roman frontiers crumbled and the emperor fell when the barbarian hordes swept in from the north and east. Goths and Vandals, followed by Mongols and Tartars from the Asian steppes, spread death and destruction throughout the civilized world. Europe entered a period of decay and anarchy from which it was not to recover for five long centuries. Periods of relative stability relieved the gloom, as the barbarians became gradually absorbed by the indigenous populations; but these periods seldom lasted for long, as one wave of invaders succeeded another.

The effect of successive barbarian onslaughts on the world of learning was catastrophic. Amid the general decline of learning, schools of philosophy, including the Epicurean school and the Academy of Plato, were closed by an edict of the Emperor Justinian (527–565) in 529. While Christians held fast to their faith, they produced no new ideas. The last of the "ancient" philosophers was the Roman poet Boethius (about 475–525), who wrote *The Consolation of Philosophy* in 524 while in prison awaiting execution for treason.

For five centuries, until the birth of Anselm in 1033, the only philosopher of note was the ninth-century Neoplatonist, Johannes Scotus Erigena (about 810–877). An Irish scholar, his best known work, written in Greek, was called *On the Divisions of Nature*. In it, he upheld the view that universals such as whiteness and roundness have an existence independent of the particular things, such as white and round objects, in which they exhibit themselves. This view found expression a few centuries later in the medieval realist school.

The Dark Ages saw the rise of monasteries. The

Left: Charles the Bald of France who appointed Irish philosopher Johannes Scotus Erigena as head of his court school in A.D. 843. Here Erigena became involved in a theological dispute and only escaped punishment because of his friendship with the king.

monastic movement originated in Egypt in the early part of the fourth century and was introduced to Christianity and the West by Athanasius (p. 102). The monasteries became the accepted repositories for learning until the universities took over this role early in the Middle Ages. Particularly important were those in Ireland which, geographically isolated, escaped the mainstream of wars, and the Italian monasteries which sprang up after Benedict founded Monte Cassino in 520 (p. 60).

The Dark Ages came to an end around the beginning of the 11th century, largely because of the pressure of a reformed Church on a society that had absorbed the last of its invaders and craved for peace. The threads of philosophy were picked up again after 500 years, but philosophy was not to be as free as in the time of the Greeks. Medieval man was allowed to speculate only within the framework of the system the Church prescribed.

Below: A 17th-century engraving of the Abbey of St. Riquier, France. This monastery was under Charlemagne's patronage. After the decay of the secular schools, the arts of reading, writing and education in general, were kept alive by such monasteries.

Arabian Philosophers

Above: Averroës, the Arabian philosopher who was a commentator on Aristotle's works. Arab thinkers like Averroës rediscovered Aristotle for the West.
Top left: a page from a 13th-century illuminated manuscript of the *Mishnah* Torah of Maimonides (1195–1204), who was the greatest of the medieval Jewish philosophers. He believed that man could only know God's works, not his nature, and also that only the intellectual part of the soul was immortal.
Bottom left: a page from a medieval Arabic version of Aristotle's biological work *De Historia Animalium*. In the Arabian world, in contrast to medieval Europe, the study of Greek science and philosophy was pursued separately from the study of theological matters.

The Moslems had no Dark Ages, a fact which enabled them to steal a march over the Christians where the interpretation of Aristotle was concerned. When the Greek philosopher's logic was required to support Christian teachings in the early Middle Ages, his works had to be read, for the most part, in Latin translations of Arabic versions. This was regarded as a serious danger to the faith, since both Avicenna and Averroës, the two great Moslem commentators on Aristotle, held views which contradicted Christian doctrine on a number of points.

Avicenna (980–1037) was born in Bukhara (now part of the Soviet Union) and taught medicine and philosophy in the legendary city of Isfahan before settling in Teheran, Persia. He hardly corresponded to the popular idea of either a doctor or a philosopher. He had a passion for wine and women and lived an extraordinary life, sometimes in palaces because of his medical services to Arabian princes, sometimes in prisons.

In his youth, Avicenna, who was brought up on the Koran, also came under the influence of Greek philosophy. Like Plotinus (p. 98), he believed in a First Cause, God, from whom emanated a series of Intelligences which animated the celestial bodies. These Intelligences in turn gave rise to Souls, which descended through the soul of the moon to the souls of humans. The element of Neoplatonism in Avicenna's thinking was thus very strong.

Avicenna also made a distinction, later of great importance to Christian scholastics, between what was called essence and existence. An essence is simply a quality which characterizes all the members of a group. For example, the color white is an essence which characterizes different white things. Existence, although present in individual things, is something which might or might not accompany essence. The nature of swans might be established by defining their essence, but it would not necessarily follow that swans exist. This distinction between essence and existence derived from Plato's theory of forms, which were supposed to reveal themselves in the particular things of which the world is made. The same problem in the terms of Christian scholastics was called the relationship between universals and particulars (p. 112).

The second great Arabian philosopher was the Spaniard Averroës (about 1126–98), who was born and lived in Cordoba. As Aristotle was known to medieval thinkers simply as "The Philosopher," so Averroës was known for his writings about the texts of Aristotle as "The Commentator." He also gave Aristotle's philosophy a Neoplatonic twist, but he denied that existence could be treated apart from essence. Averroës, whose views on eternity led to the burning of his books by Moslem theologians, did not picture the Creation as a single act, but as an ever-continuing process in a changing cosmos. Averroës had a great vision of harmony between the heavens and the earth. He related everything that happened on earth to the Prime Mover, God.

Arabic Spain was also the birthplace of the great Jewish thinker, Moses Maimonides (1135–1204), who went to Cairo when he was 30 and remained there for the rest of his life. He wrote a book called *The Guide for the Perplexed*, which attempted to reconcile the teachings of Judaism with Aristotle. Like Averroës, Maimonides believed God's existence could be proved by argument, but he also believed God could be known through revelation, and that faith and reason are different forms of knowledge. He got into trouble with orthodox Jewry, which denounced him as a heretic, but his ideas influenced Thomas Aquinas.

Below: Jewish scholars of the Middle Ages belonged chiefly to the Arabian tradition. An Eastern ruler (left) hands an Arabic original to a Jewish translator who is seen (right) giving the Latin version to Charles of Anjou. Jewish philosophy mediated between Christian and Moslem thought and was often in Arabic, not Hebrew.

Thomas Aquinas

Thomas Aquinas (about 1225–74), the greatest of the scholastics (p. 112), was born of a noble Lombard family in a castle near a little village between Naples and Rome. He went first to an abbey for his schooling and then to the University of Naples, where he entered the Dominican Order. Later he traveled in Europe and studied in Paris and Cologne under Albertus Magnus (about 1193–1280), the leading Aristotelian of the day, before finally returning to Italy to teach theology.

People who follow St. Thomas' philosophy are known as Thomists. Thomism is not the sole Roman Catholic philosophy, as is sometimes thought, but it is certainly the most important. Aquinas' two major works, the *Summa Theologica* and the *Summa Contra Gentiles* (Against the Heathens) still form a valuable guide to Roman Catholic thought. In these books Aquinas tried to justify the Christian religion by combining theology with Aristotelian philosophy. The earlier scholastics had thought Plato more important than Aristotle, but Aquinas persuaded the Church that the converse was true, and also that his own interpretation of Aristotle was to be preferred to that of the Arabian philosophers and their Christian followers. He did accept Avicenna's distinction between essence and existence (p. 109). However, Aquinas said the distinction cannot be made in the case of God. In him existence and essence coincide.

A problem which particularly interested Aquinas was the distinction between faith and reason. He argued that faith is more comprehensive than reason, for while some truths can be proved by reason, they can also be known by faith and other means as well. Among the truths that can be proved by reason are the existence of God and the immortality of the soul. Among the truths that cannot be proved are the Incarnation, the resurrection of the body and the doctrine of the Trinity.

Regarding the wide range of problems connected with sin, God's grace and predestination, Aquinas took much the same line as Augustine. He considered evil to be a privation, not created directly by God, but consisting in the absence of good in much the same way as blindness consists in the absence of sight. Evil results from man's failure to will the good and occurs because men have free will.

Aquinas believed that God can be known either through reason or revelation. He rejected the so-called ontological proof of God's existence given by Anselm (1033–1109), according to which God, being perfect, must exist. If he did not, he would lack the quality of existence and so would not be perfect. But Aquinas produced no fewer than five different arguments to prove the existence of God. The most famous is the First Mover argument, which implies that it is impossible for a series to extend backwards indefinitely in time. There are things in the world which move about and things which move them. If we go backwards in time, since an object's natural state is one of rest, it follows that we must eventually arrive at an Unmoved Mover. This is God.

It was only prior to the English scientist Sir Isaac Newton (p. 116) that philosophers thought an object's natural state was one of rest. Newton's First Law of Motion states that is is natural for an object to continue in the state it is *in*, whether moving or at rest. So Newton's First Law destroys Aquinas' premise. However, even if Aquinas' argument were valid, it would still be necessary to prove that the First Cause is God. The world might well have been created by Descartes' malevolent demon (p. 119). Aquinas did not dispute the logical possibility that the world might have existed forever. He simply argued that it could not have done so in fact, because it would be impossible for existing objects to have had no prior cause.

Thomas Triumphant, a painting by Francesco Traini (about 1346). Aquinas is seated between Plato and Aristotle, with the defeated Arabian Averroës lying at his feet. Averroës had endeavored to separate science and theology, whereas Aquinas tried to effect a synthesis between Greek logic and science and the Christian faith. He spent most of his short life teaching theology in Italy.

ARISTOTILES
PLATO
ritatem meditabitur i guttur meum
et labia mea detestabuntur impiū.

Scholasticism

Above: St. Francis, born about 1182 in Assisi, Umbria, in Italy. The founder of the Franciscan order, he believed that nature was the reflection of God: his affection for all creatures and love of poverty and simplicity followed naturally. After his death in 1226 the Franciscan order spread rapidly throughout all of Europe.

The learned men of the Middle Ages were called scholastics. The great period of scholastic thought was from about 1100 to 1500. The main philosophical problems of this time centered around the difference between "universals" and "particulars," proofs of the existence of God, and faith and reason.

The question about universals was whether general concepts such as whiteness, humanity and justice are notions of the mind without anything corresponding to them in the outside world, or whether they have a reality outside human thought. Plato's forms (p. 92) are universals. Plato's theory is a form of *realism:* Universals have a real, objective existence outside the particular objects in which they are manifested. The alternative realist explanation of universals was that of Aristotle, who believed that universals exist, but within the objects which they characterize, not outside them.

The realist theory dominated philosophical thought until the late Middle Ages. It was upheld by Erigena, Avicenna and Aquinas. Nevertheless, beginning in the 11th century, philosophers began to think of universals in different ways, and in the ensuing centuries two trends emerged: *nominalism* and *conceptualism.*

Nominalists believed that universals have no objective existence at all. They are simply words naming a number of similar things. The existence of such general words does not entail the existence of the general things named. One of the early nominalists was Roscellinus (1050–1125). William of Ockham (about 1300–49) was one of the most thoroughgoing nominalists. He said that only particulars exist. Therefore, essences, forms and ideas are unnecessary and should be abandoned. This belief is the source of the principle called "Ockham's razor," which states that theoretical entities should not be needlessly multiplied.

Above: Duns Scotus and two pupils, from a 14th-century manuscript. He was a Franciscan critic of St. Thomas Aquinas and taught that faith was superior to reason, which was denied by Aquinas. Born in Scotland, He taught at Oxford, Paris and Cologne.

Conceptualists took a position between realism and nominalism. They believed that universals are more than mere words, but they have a purely abstract reality as notions of the mind. If the human race were destroyed, universals would be destroyed as well. A man who attempted a synthesis of the nominalist and conceptualist opinions, but who leaned towards the latter, was Peter Abélard (1079–1142). He was at one time a pupil of Roscellinus.

The scholastics opposing Aquinas were also

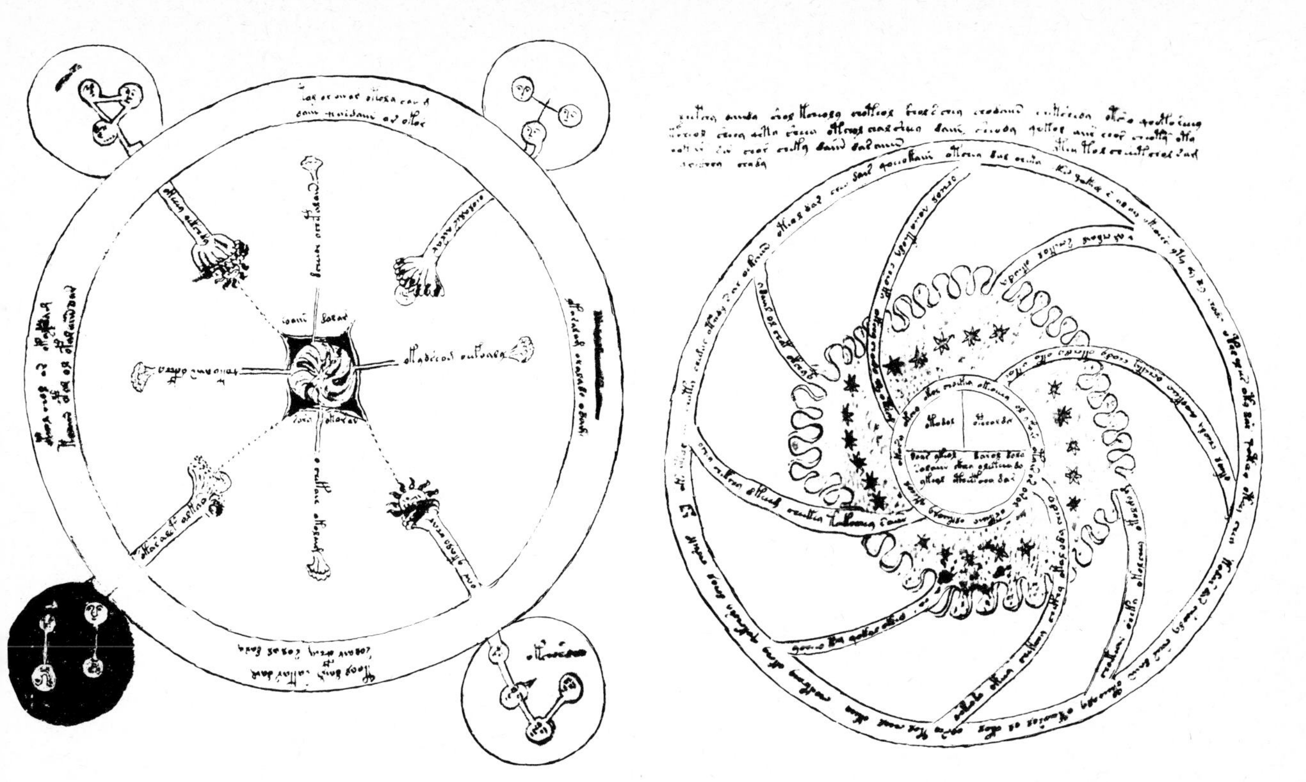

Above: an account of eclipses and comets from an early manuscript of Roger Bacon (1214–94), a Franciscan friar opposed to the tradition of St. Thomas Aquinas. He worked in Oxford and Paris, studying all branches of learning. He held that reason based on experiments should be the foundation of all sciences, except that of theology, which depends on divine authority. His beliefs cost him 15 years in prison.

concerned with separating faith and reason. They were trying to free theology from Greek philosophy, and philosophy from theology. They thought theology is a matter of faith alone and cannot be given rational support by philosophy. The existence of God cannot be proved by reason; we can only believe in him.

One man who challenged the authority of Aquinas' teachings was Roger Bacon (about 1214–94), who believed that man should experiment to obtain knowledge rather than turn back to Aristotle. His views were condemned and he was sentenced to 15 years in prison.

The Scottish Franciscan Duns Scotus (about 1265–1308) also challenged the accepted link between philosophy and theology. He believed reason to be of little use in matters of theology. He denied that there are two kinds of being, essence and existence, as Aquinas thought. Since being can be caused, there must be a first being. The first being would have to be uncaused and therefore infinite. This is God. Duns Scotus said that God's uniqueness is his divine will, not a special kind of existence. Good exists since God wills it. Duns Scotus disagreed with Aquinas that God simply recognizes the good through his wisdom.

Scholasticism became less important after the 15th century, but the debates over universals and particulars and faith and reason did much to prepare the way for modern science and philosophy.

Below left: William of Ockham (about 1300–49), who led the break with the Thomist tradition, and helped open the way for empiricism. Below right: a page from a 14th-century version of Ockham's work, *Summa Totius Logices*, in which he separated reason from faith.

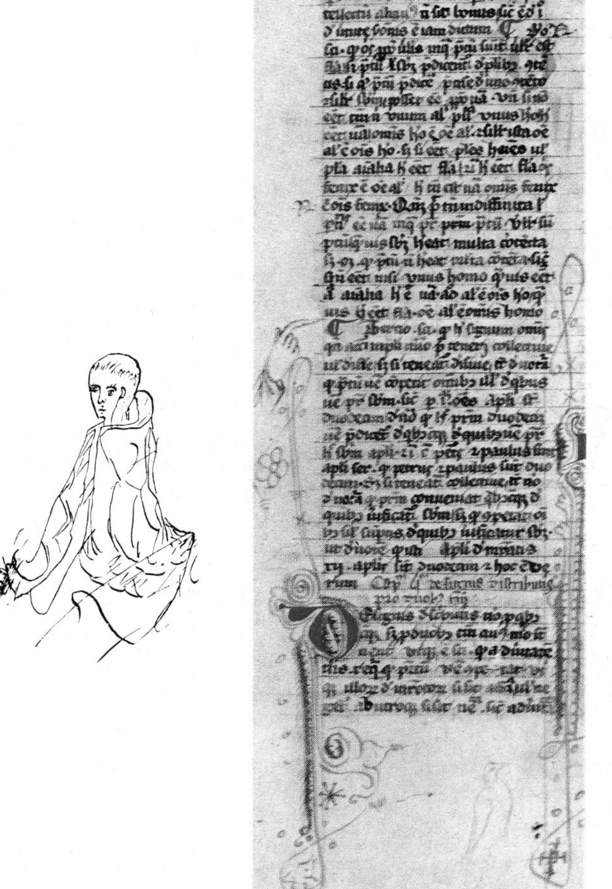

This 17th-century picture shows
the sun-centered universe of the Polish astronomer, Copernicus.
Proceeding outwards from the sun are the orbits
and signs of Mercury, Venus, the Earth, Mars, Jupiter and Saturn.
Uranus, Neptune and Pluto were still to be discovered.
It took about a century for Copernicus' discovery
to become widely accepted. When it was,
it revolutionized astronomy.

THE RISE OF MODERN PHILOSOPHY

With the rise of the new science, heralded by the discoveries of Copernicus and Galileo, the predominance of the Church began to decline. The Church had encouraged philosophy but had held it captive. Now philosophy became more oriented toward the secular world. Two major traditions developed: rationalism, the view that reason is the only source of knowledge; and empiricism, the view that knowledge comes from experience.

The New Spirit

The prescriptions of the Church, together with the lack of any modern experimental methods in science and too great a readiness to accept the authority of Plato and Aristotle in philosophy, created a certain rigidity in medieval thought. Debates among the scholastics began to break down some of the accepted ways of thinking, and the controversies anticipated two developments of the 16th century which were to revolutionize man's way of thinking about the world: the rise of modern science and a change of emphasis and direction in philosophy itself.

A large part of the authority and prestige of the Church during medieval times derived from the belief that the earth was of special importance in the cosmic scheme. God was supposed to have carefully positioned it at the center of the universe, with the sun and other heavenly bodies revolving around it. Nicolaus Copernicus (1473–1543), Johannes Kepler (1571–1630) and Galileo Galilei (1564–1642), however, disputed this. Far from remaining motionless at the center of things, they said, the earth is both rotating on its axis and revolving around the sun.

Copernicus recognized that his discoveries would be opposed by the Church, and delayed publication of his findings until 1543, the year of his death. They were published quietly and came to the attention only of fellow mathematicians. One of these was Kepler, a German astronomer and astrologer, who spent the rest of his life working out mathematical proofs of Copernicus' discoveries. Galileo was forced by the Inquisition to repudiate his theories under a threat of torture (although, according to legend, after assuring the Inquisition that the earth is still, he said under his breath, "nevertheless it moves"). But Copernicus, Kepler and Galileo succeeded in giving science a mathematical orientation, even though the Church's

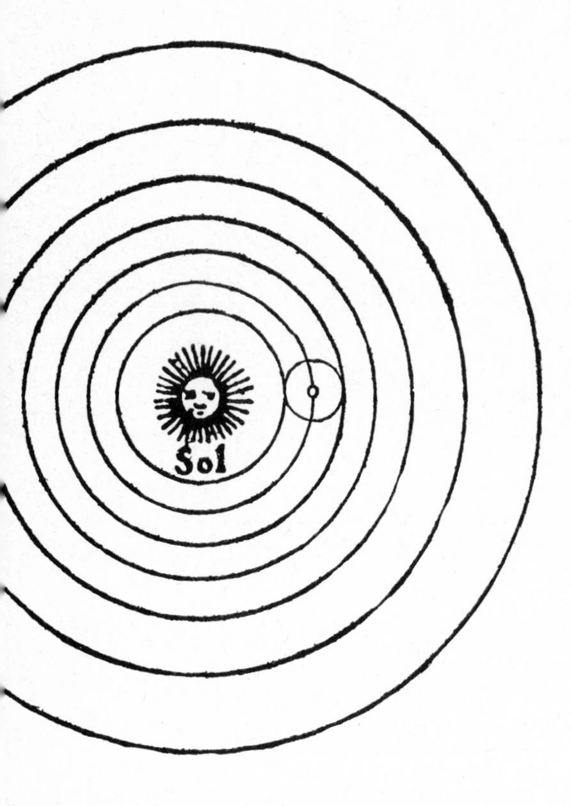

Above: Galileo Galilei (1564–1642) was condemned by the Church for supporting the Copernican theory in his work *Dialogue on the Two Chief World Systems, the Ptolemaic and the Copernican.*

Above: a rough sketch of the Copernican sun-centered universe. Below: Nicolaus Copernicus was born in Polish Pomerania in 1473. He was educated by the Church, which taught the then-accepted Ptolemaic astronomy. His own heliocentric theory later replaced this.

opposition meant that Italy gave up its initiative in the new scientific pursuit to northern Europe.

The new scientific outlook culminated in the work of Sir Isaac Newton (1642–1727), a scientific giant who brought together various earlier strands of inquiry into a single whole. Before he was 25, Newton had discovered the binomial theorem, differential and integral calculus (independently of Leibniz, p. 120), the mathematical movement of the planets and the law of universal gravitation. Albert Einstein (1879–1955) said of Newton's work generally that he had achieved "perhaps the greatest intellectual stride that it has been granted to any man to make."

The rise of modern science, then, was one of the main causes of the passing of the medieval era. Science became mathematically oriented and scientists began to concentrate on the inductive method, testing their hypotheses by observation and experi-

Above: Copernicus' room at Frauenberg, where he was a canon.
Right: the frontispiece of Galileo's *Dialogue*, showing Aristotle, Ptolemy and Copernicus together. Galileo was later forced by the Inquisition to renounce his belief in the heliocentric universe.

ments, and formulating natural laws from them.

There were also changes within philosophy itself. Medieval philosophy was dominated by Aristotelianism and Roman Catholic doctrine, which again the scholastic debates had begun to break down. In the 15th century, philosophers began to think increasingly in terms of the natural world. There was less and less speculation about metaphysical entities like essences and universals. In the 16th and 17th centuries, men began to see nature as a machine and to explain the world in mechanical terms.

While philosophy asserted its independence of theology, it did not turn against religion. Philosophers like Descartes (p. 118) considered spirit to be separate from matter, thereby accepting the new scientific findings without rejecting religion. But reason was no longer used simply as a tool for proving theological beliefs.

DISCOURS
DE LA METHODE
Pour bien conduire ſa raiſon & chercher la verité dans les ſciences.
PLUS
LA DIOPTRIQVE.
LES METEORES.
ET
LA GEOMETRIE.
Qui ſont des eſſais de cete METHODE.

A LEYDE
De l'Imprimerie de IAN MAIRE.
cIↃ IↃ c xxxvII.
Auec Priuilege.

Modern philosophy begins with René Descartes (1596–1650), whose philosophy begins with his famous statement *Cogito, ergo sum* (I think, therefore I am). Descartes reached this conclusion after a lengthy inquiry into the things it is possible to know without doubt. First he considered ordinary experiences. Could he doubt, for example, that he was sitting by the fire in his dressing gown? Yes, he could, for he might be dreaming. Admittedly, it was not very likely, but that was not the point. He was concerned only with what is certain beyond the remotest possibility of mistake.

Above: a portrait of René Descartes (1596–1650) who, in his work *Discourse on Method*, presented his four rules of logic. They were as follows: first, only to accept clear and distinct ideas; second, to divide problems into as many parts as possible; third, to begin with the simplest problems and move gradually to the complex; fourth, to be careful that all parts of the problem were enumerated and that none had been left out.

Right: the title page and statement of the four precepts, from a facsimile of the first edition which was published in 1637.

20 DISCOURS.

Le premier eſtoit de ne receuoir iamais aucune choſe pour vraye que ie ne la connuſſe euidemment eſtre telle: c'eſt à dire, d'euiter ſoigneuſement la Precipitation, & la Preuention; & de ne comprendre rien de plus en mes iugemens, que ce qui ſe preſenteroit ſi clairement & ſi diſtinctement a mon eſprit, que ie n'euſſe aucune occaſion de le mettre en doute.

Le ſecond, de diuiſer chaſcune des difficultez que i'examinerois en autant de parcelles qu'il ſe pourroit, & qu'il ſeroit requis pour les mieux reſoudre.

Le troiſieſme de conduire par ordre mes penſées, en commenceant par les obiets les plus ſimples, & les plus ayſez a connoiſtre, pour monter peu a peu comme par degrez iuſques a la connoiſſance des plus compoſez: Et ſuppoſant meſme de l'ordre entre ceux qui ne ſe precedent point naturellement les vns les autres.

Et le dernier de faire partout des denombremens ſi entiers, & des reueuës ſi generales, que ie fuſſe aſſuré de ne rien omettre.

Right: Queen Christina of Sweden, who in 1649, persuaded Descartes to come to Stockholm to teach her. She insisted that he give her philosophy lessons at five o'clock in the morning. Descartes, who was unaccustomed to the Swedish winter and to rising before noon, could not endure it. He died of a chill early in 1650.

Next, Descartes considered the truths of mathematics. Surely he could not doubt that two and two equal four. But he decided he could, for there had been occasions in the past when he had made mistakes in mathematics. How could he be sure that he was not making one now? Descartes even supposed it was possible—since he could not deny it with certainty—that the world had been created, not by God, but by a malevolent demon who amused himself by deceiving philosophers about truth and falsity. But he found there remained one thing which, try as he might, he could not doubt. He could not doubt that he, who had these doubts, existed, at least while he was having them. His conclusion is often simply referred to as the Cogito, and the process by which it was reached is called Cartesian doubt.

Descartes now had a sure foundation on which he could build. Using the Cogito as an explorer might use a base camp, as a place to set out from, Descartes proceeded to argue from it. He was convinced of the existence of God because he had an idea of a perfect Being which he could not account for unless a perfect Being had caused it. From God he argued back to the existence of the world and other people. Other people certainly *seem* to exist, and Descartes thought it was scarcely credible that the Creator would have deceived him. He used God to bridge the gap between his mind and the outside world.

Descartes' argument from God to the existence of the world is a weak one. But the Cogito still stands and is very important. If it is valid (and no one has clearly refuted it), Descartes has cut us off from the outside world. However probable it may be that other people exist, it can never be entirely certain that they do. The absurdity of this conclusion, coupled with the seeming impossibility of refuting it, has troubled generations of philosophers.

Nor was this the only problem which Descartes handed on to later philosophers. He made a distinction between mind and body, according to which the body exists in space but the mind does not. Tables and chairs, for example, can be measured, but thoughts cannot be. The problem then arose, how can something which does not occupy space affect something which does? How can the brain, which is material, be affected by thoughts, which are not? Given this view, it is as absurd to think that thoughts can cause bodily movements as it is to believe they can cause movements of things at a distance, just by willing. The problem of the exact relationship between mind and body has never been solved in the terms in which Descartes posed it.

In addition to being a philosopher, Descartes was a brilliant mathematician. When he was only 23, for example, he discovered that algebra and geometry could be coordinated to form one science by plotting equations along rectangular axes. In an essay called "Meteors," Descartes gave one of the first scientific explanations of the weather. He also made valuable contributions to musical theory and physics. In fact, Cartesian physics rivaled Newtonian physics for more than a century. However, Descartes' standing in these fields does not approach his importance as a philosopher.

Leibniz and Spinoza

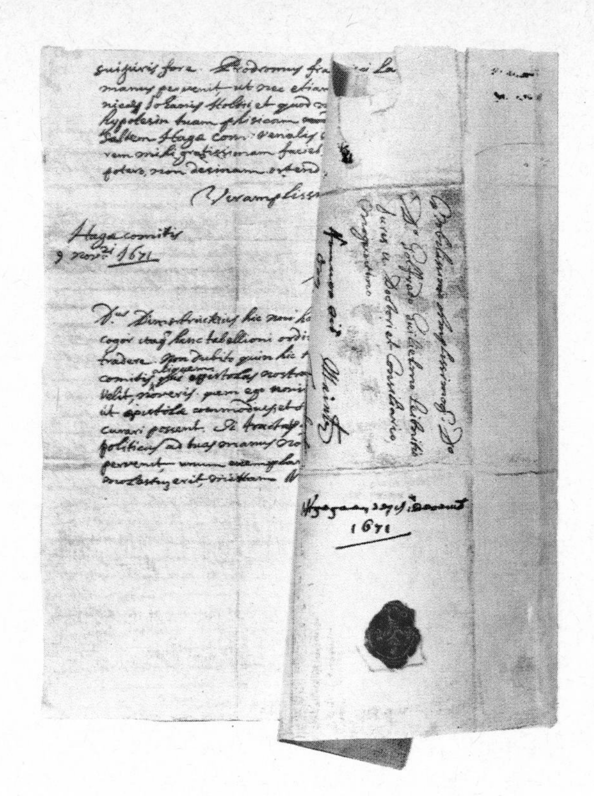

Above: a letter from Spinoza concerning his *Theologico-Political Treatise* (1670). In this work Spinoza pleads for toleration, arguing that the value of religion lies not in its truth but in its effect on human behavior.

Gottfried Wilhelm von Leibniz (1646–1716) flashed across the philosophic scene with the brilliance of a shooting star. One of the greatest pure intellects of whom we have any record, he discovered integral and differential calculus and constructed a calculating machine. He dreamed of creating a universal logic. He advised scientists in almost every field. He was a lawyer, historian and theologian. He became the secretary of the secret society of the Rosicrucians. Whenever he got the chance, he advised kings and princes on diplomacy, and he was prepared to advise generals on how to plan their military campaigns. He was always willing to help people less talented than himself.

In philosophy Leibniz had a curious theory. He thought the universe consists of an infinite number of simple, immaterial substances called *monads*, which do not interact with one another. Things seem to interact, certainly, but that is only because, at the beginning of time, God wound up all the monads like a number of clocks and started them off in time with one another. They have kept time ever since. Why do a man's legs move when he decides to go for a walk? Because of the previous states of the monads composing them. That is a simple causal relationship. Parallel with this relationship, and in harmony with it, the monads with which the man thinks decide to go for a walk. They do this because of some past condition in *their* state. There is thus no interaction between mind and body. Leibniz called the principle of parallel movements "pre-established harmony," and he held the Creator responsible for it.

Another interesting theory of Leibniz's was that this is the "best of all possible worlds." By this he meant that of the infinite number of worlds which it is possible to imagine, God chose this particular world because it has the greatest possible surplus of good over evil.

Baruch Spinoza (1632–77), who, like Leibniz, was a rationalist deeply influenced by René Descartes, arrived at very different conclusions about the

Leibniz believed that the universe was planned by God and that God-given rules controlled everything, down to the possible combinations of dryness, heat, dampness and cold, as shown in this diagram of his.

Right: Gottfried Wilhelm von Leibniz. His well-known works include *Theodicy, Monadology* and *Discourse on Metaphysics.* Leibniz was active in so many fields that some of his most important writings are only fragmentary notes, correspondence and short essays.

Above: Baruch Spinoza (1632–77), a Jew of Portuguese origin who lived in Holland, was a monist and believed God and nature to be identical. Spinoza was denounced as an atheist during his life and his chief work, *Ethics*, was published anonymously after his death.

world. Whereas Leibniz was a pluralist, believing there are a great many different things in the world, Spinoza was a monist. He believed the world is just one substance. Leibniz believed that God is outside the universe; Spinoza believed God *is* the universe, a view which is called pantheism.

Spinoza thought God is nature and nature, God. Nature has an infinite number of attributes, of which man perceives only two, namely mind and matter. Nature is what Spinoza called a substance, by which he meant that it is self-subsistent, or "conceived through itself." Men, on the other hand, and most of the things they deal with in their everyday lives, are what Spinoza called *modes*. Modes are dependent for their existence on something else, and are completely determined by their causal relations to the rest of the world. Men think that they are free, but this is an illusion arising from their ignorance of the real causes acting on them. This led Spinoza to his central thesis that man should practice the "intellectual love of God," not from fear, or from false desire to please, but because this is the same thing as understanding the interrelationship of everything in nature, including oneself.

Spinoza is extremely difficult to read. He tried to establish his conclusions as if he were writing a geometry book, beginning with a series of definitions and axioms and continuing with the theorems and corollaries deducible from them. He thought the universe could be discussed in the same way as mathematics.

Bacon, Hobbes and Locke

Above: John Locke (1632–1704), a common-sense philosopher, is generally regarded as the originator of modern empiricism. He believed that to discover and solve the world's problems one must go out and look, rather than try to draw valid conclusions by the use of pure reason alone.

Francis Bacon (1561–1626) was a lawyer, statesman and philosopher. He entered Parliament at the age of 23. In 1618 he became Lord Chancellor of England but was dismissed from his post two years later for accepting bribes. This he admitted, claiming only that accepting them never affected his legal judgments. The law's loss, however, proved science's gain, for the termination of his political career gave Bacon the time he needed to formulate the ideas on scientific method which have made him famous.

The essence of Bacon's method was observation and experiment. He stressed the importance of inductive as opposed to deductive reasoning (p. 94), and as a result he has been called the father of English science. He had great faith in the future of science and was one of the few to realize the benefits it could bring to humanity, properly used. In *The Advancement of Learning*, Bacon argued that knowledge brings power—and the knowledge he had in mind was scientific. He also believed in God, thinking his existence could be proved by reason, a common belief among intellectuals of the time.

Thomas Hobbes (1586–1679) was Bacon's secretary as a young man and his philosophical thought reflects Bacon's influence. Hobbes was a thoroughgoing materialist who reduced the whole life of the mind to physical motions. The future of mankind is predictable, according to this theory.

Hobbes' best-known work was *Leviathan*, a book on political theory. Whereas bees in a hive cooperate naturally, argued Hobbes, men in a society cooperate only to avoid the fighting that would break out among them otherwise. Men give up the state of nature when they create a governing body to rule

A 15th-century Flemish painting showing a man consulting a witch. Traditional beliefs in the power of magic and witchcraft still persisted in the late Middle Ages throughout the civilized world. Francis Bacon in his *Novum Organum* condemned such beliefs because of their stifling effect on the spirit of true scientific inquiry.

This medallion of 1621 shows Francis Bacon (1561–1626) as Viscount St. Albans and the Lord Chancellor of England. Both statesman and philosopher, Bacon helped to give science its modern experimental method.

them, and they must obey its laws in return for protection of their lives and property.

John Locke (1632–1704) was the founder of modern empiricism, which is the view that all knowledge is derived from experience, rather than deduced from rationally certain principles. Bacon's method was also empirical, but Locke was the first to give a detailed philosophic exposition of the origin in experience of our ideas and beliefs.

Locke's opinions are set forth in his *Essay Concerning Human Understanding*, which Voltaire once remarked was "understood by everyone except philosophers." In it, Locke attacked the vague but widely-held rationalist belief that at birth the mind already has a certain amount of knowledge which it then applies to problems as they arise. This was known as the theory of "innate ideas." Locke argued that at birth the mind is like a sheet of white paper, devoid of all knowledge. Sensory experience—seeing, tasting, feeling, hearing, smelling—provides the basis of simple ideas. Our minds reflect on these simple ideas and form more complex ones from them.

Locke also has had considerable influence as a political philosopher. In the second of his *Two Treatises on Government*, he wrote that government began as a social contract and is therefore a public trust which can be withdrawn if those in power betray the trust. Although the idea of a social contract is now discredited, Locke's ideas had great impact in an age when kings were thought to rule by divine right. The treatises were written to refute that idea and to justify the English Revolution of 1688 which placed William III on the throne. Locke's belief that the powers of the legislature and the executive should be separate greatly influenced the framers of the United States Constitution, and is reflected in the division between the legislative, executive and judicial branches of the government today.

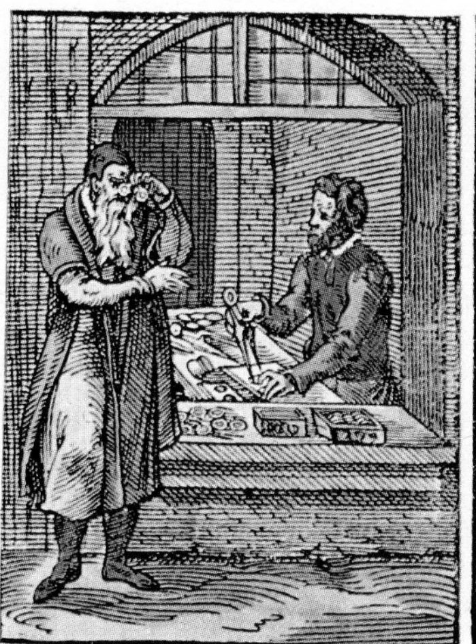

Above: Bacon thought that man should be the "servant and interpreter of nature" which, if rightly understood, would enable him to improve his way of life. The 16th-century engravings show (left to right), an optician, a merchant, a printer and an apothecary. Bacon appears to have seen his own role as considerably less ordinary. He pictured himself as an overlord of the various fields of science, taking all knowledge as his province, and magnanimously prepared to give advice to anyone who needed it, in the manner of a later German philosopher, Leibniz.

Bishop Berkeley

Bishop George Berkeley (1685–1753) (portrait below), was born in Ireland and educated at Trinity College, Dublin. Before he was 30 years old he had published the philosophic works on which his fame rests. The first of these was *An Essay Towards A New Theory of Vision* (1709), the title page of which is shown (below left). In this, Berkeley argued that we do not perceive distance by sight, for distance is a line the end of which cannot be seen by the eye. He believed we *judge* distance in various ways. In his *Principles of Human Knowledge* (a section of the manuscript appears below, far right) he set out his basic theory. Here he reveals himself as an idealist, because he believed that the real world consists of minds and their sensations and ideas. Idealism is the opposite of realism, the belief that the world has an objective existence apart from the mind. To him, therefore, the things we see depend for their existence on the mind of the observer. This concept he expressed in his famous statement, "to be is to be perceived." If we look at a red carpet, then turn our eyes away, is the redness still in the carpet or was it only in us? Berkeley's view was that not only the redness but the whole carpet would cease to exist if no one were observing it. It is interesting to compare Berkeley's theory with that of Newton and Locke. The philosophy of classical physics was that the primary qualities of the carpet, its extension, solidity and shape, exist in nature. Its secondary qualities, like texture and color, although they are dependent for their existence on the primary qualities, exist only in the mind. Berkeley, on the other hand, thought that primary qualities were no more objective, and no less, than secondary qualities. Philonous, a character in one of Berkeley's dialogues, expresses the view thus: "I see this cherry, I feel it, I taste it: and I am sure that 'nothing' cannot be seen, or felt, or tasted: it is therefore real. Take away the sensations of softness, moisture, redness, tartness, and you take away the cherry." The space the cherry occupied could also be taken away. There was, however, an obvious objection to Berkeley's theory. It was all very well to say that a room, for example, only existed through being perceived. But what happened if no one was there to perceive it. Did the room disappear? Berkeley found a solution which fitted very well with his faith. If objects were not to go out of existence whenever human beings stopped looking at them, the objects would have to continue to be perceived by a greater mind than man's. This gave Bishop Berkeley his proof of God's existence, and it was his aim to revive belief in God. In connection with his project to found a college in Bermuda, he spent the years 1728–31 in Rhode Island, where he is shown (right) with his wife and friends.

AN

ESSAY

Towards a

New Theory

OF

VISION.

By George Berkeley, M. A.
Fellow of *Trinity College, Dublin.*

DUBLIN:

Printed by Aaron Rhames, at the Back of *Dick's Coffee-House*, for Jeremy Pepyat, Bookseller in *Skinner-Row*, MDCCIX.

~~of matter~~ Whether Corporeal Substance ~~can~~ think,
whether Matter be infinitely divisible and how it can
operate on Spirit, ~~& how motion is com~~ these
and the like ~~Subtilty~~ inquiries have given infinite amuse-
ment to Philosophers in all ages. but depending
~~they being~~ on the existence of Matter, they ~~being~~ have
no ~~place~~ longer any place on our Principles. Many other
advantages there ~~are~~ are as well with regard to Religion
as ye Sciences which ~~evidently~~ ~~[illegible]~~ it

Hume

David Hume (1711–76) was one of the principal British empiricists, along with Locke and Berkeley, both of whom influenced Hume's thought. Locke believed that the mind has ideas, caused by "material" objects. Berkeley believed that there are no material objects, only the mind's ideas of them. Hume did not even believe that there is such a thing as mind, only bundles of perceptions or ideas with no underlying unity.

The commonsense view of the self assumes that it is a permanent entity which endures through change. George may be in a good mood today and have been in a bad temper yesterday, but George remains the same person. It was precisely this assumption that Hume questioned. He pointed out that if we try to discover and examine this self or soul we are supposed to have, we fail to find it. "For my part," Hume said, "when I enter most intimately into what I call *myself*, I always stumble on some particular perception or other, of heat or cold, light or shade, love or hatred, pain or pleasure. I never catch *myself* at any time without a perception."

Perhaps, however, the self is something hidden away, so that it would be useless to expect intro-

Above: David Hume (1711–76), who published Parts I and II of his *Treatise of Human Nature* in 1739. It attracted even less attention than had Locke's *Essay*, some 50 years before. Yet these two works were to be the starting point for British empirical philosophy.

Below: Edinburgh in Hume's time. Hume, who was a historian as well as a philosopher, went to the University of Edinburgh at the age of 12. He studied in France but eventually returned to be the librarian at the University of Scotland—a position he fully enjoyed.

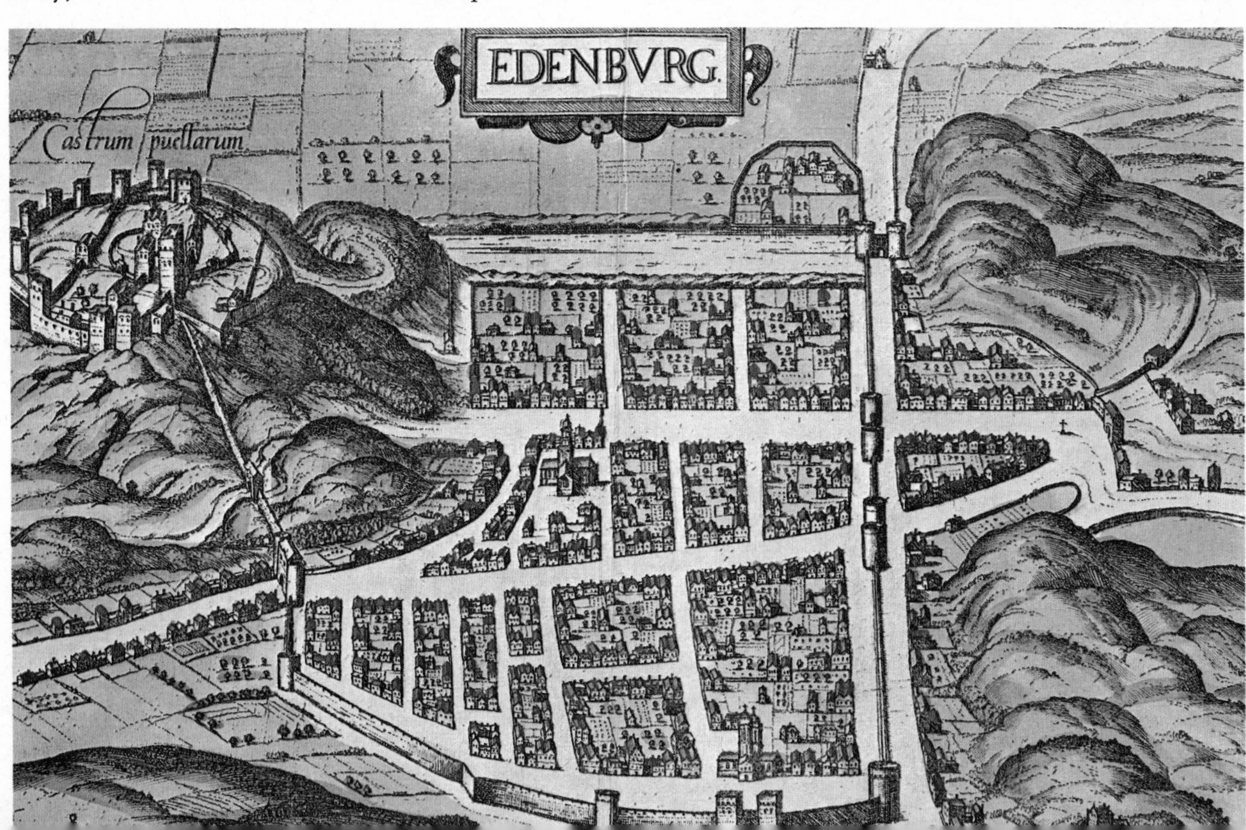

spection to reveal it? But in that case, said Hume, we should at least be able to form an idea of what it is like. We cannot. We have to imagine something that would be always the same and yet which is quite unlike anything we experience in particular sensations. Yet Hume failed to notice, when he said "I never catch myself," that the "I" which fails to find itself must be presupposed even in describing the attempt. Expecting the mind to observe itself is perhaps like expecting the eye to see itself.

Another problem to receive Hume's skeptical attention was causation, which he treated in much the same manner as he had dealt with the self. Just as the majority of people assume they have permanent selves, so they take it for granted that there is a necessary connection between cause and effect. Ordinary language implicitly admits this assumption by its use of words like "power" and "force," while experience seems to bear it out in a thousand and one ways. Who has not had the feeling, while watching a rocket rise slowly and majestically from its launching pad, of the almost irresistible power that is lifting it to the skies?

But Hume pointed out that in every case in which A is supposed to produce or cause B, all that anyone sees is that A is *followed* by B. Just as we have no real notion of what the self is like, so Hume argued that we have no notion of what power or necessary connection is like. All that we ever notice in the world is that like follows like. Instead of being content to describe the world in this way, we project necessity into it.

The importance of Hume's theory was that it undermined the objective basis of causation. If causes contain no forces which impose their effects, in what does the objective causal link reside? If, on the other hand, causes do *not* necessitate effects, what is there to stop the whole world from behaving quite differently in five minutes time? It is no good saying that the sun will probably continue to rise because it always has, because Hume has removed the objective links between the events of the past and those of the present. All that is left is an expectancy in human beings, due to past associations of ideas, that the future will continue to resemble the past. That expectancy is subjective and cannot be rationally justified. The objective uniformity of nature remains unexplained. This is the celebrated problem of induction, which has troubled philosophers from Hume to Bertrand Russell.

This, Dear Sir, is the last Correction I shall probably trouble you with: For Dr Black has promised me, that all shall be over with me in a very little time: This Promise he makes by his power of Prediction, not that of Prescription. And indeed I consider it as good News: For of late, within these few weeks, my Infirmities have so multiplyed, that Life has become rather a Burthen to me. Adieu, then, my good and old Friend

David Hume

Above: part of a letter from Hume to his publisher, written shortly before his death. In addition to his philosophical works, Hume wrote a number of books on epistemology, ethics and politics, including a history of England which helped make him both famous and prosperous.

Eighteenth-century France was the age of the *philosophes*, who were brilliant intellectuals and popularizers rather than philosophers in the academic sense. They delighted French salons with their conversation and outraged the conventional middle classes with their new morality. The most famous, Voltaire (p. 73), wrote on everything from the theater to abstract philosophy. It was only after his death that people began to suspect that his appearance of profundity may have been partly due to his elegant style. The calm self-assurance of Voltaire and his friends derived from their faith in science and belief in reason and human progress.

Denis Diderot (1713–84), an admirer of Locke's new empiricism, would accept nothing as true that could not be verified by the senses, thereby anticipating the logical empiricists (p. 152) by some 200 years. Etienne de Condillac (1715–80) agreed with Diderot. Claude Helvétius (1715–71) and Paul d'Holbach (1723–89) both thought of human beings as motivated almost entirely by the desire to seek pleasure and avoid pain. D'Holbach not only analyzed goodness in terms of happiness, but anticipated the English utilitarians Jeremy Bentham and John Stuart Mill, by suggesting an ethical goal of the greatest happiness of the greatest number of people (p. 139).

The 18th century also produced Jean Jacques Rousseau (1712–78), who made his name by writing an essay which denied that either the arts or the sciences had conferred benefits on mankind. Vagabond, imposter, masochist, music tutor, petty thief,

The first Festival of the Supreme Being—an event held in Paris during the French Revolution. It was intended to celebrate the triumph of the new god, Reason, over all established religion, and marked a popular victory for the ideas of the 18th-century French philosophers.

Eighteenth-century thinkers were already questioning the basis of established Christianity in 1755, when there was a catastrophic earthquake in Lisbon which claimed over 20,000 victims. This seemed to make nonsense of the Christian view that God is love. But when Voltaire said as much, he was attacked by Rousseau, who refused to see the connection between such a catastrophe and a benevolent Creator.

this extraordinary man worked his way to the top of French society. He produced a brilliant book pleading for equality in social relationships (*The Social Contract*, 1762), and was probably the first man to argue that there are better reasons for believing in God than philosophy can offer. To a woman in doubt he wrote, "Ah, Madame! Sometimes in the privacy of my study, with my hands pressed tight over my eyes or in the darkness of the night, I am of the opinion that there is no God. But look yonder: the rising of the sun, as it scatters the mists that cover the earth, and lays bare the wondrous glittering scene of nature, disperses at the same moment all cloud from my soul. I find my faith again, and my God, and my belief in him." Such sentiments were quite uncommon in the great age of confidence in reason.

Rousseau was the first important figure in the romantic movement, and he was swimming against the tide of 18th-century rationalism. The tradition of the scientifically-minded philosophes was carried on in the next century by Auguste Comte (1798–1857), the founder of modern sociology. His *Course in Positive Philosophy* argued that science would replace metaphysics as metaphysics had replaced dogmatic religion.

The Sophists of ancient Greece, the French philosophes and the American pragmatists (p. 142) who wrote in the 20th century all condemned vague speculation and wanted to see human affairs run in a practical way by scientists or their kind. Considered in this light, positivism, whether expressed by the Sophists of Greece or the logical empiricists of today, has its roots in a tradition that is older than philosophy itself. It is derived from the practical outlook of people in everyday life.

"I have a supreme aversion," wrote Comte, "to scientific labors whose utility, direct or remote, I do not see." Eventually, however, Comte came to the conclusion that science alone could not save mankind. A new religion of science was needed to replace the old "superstitions." This led Comte, living in the shadow of the French Revolution, to formulate a new religion of humanity in which man replaced God as the principal object of worship. The desires of man which should be satisfied were those of the heart, so Comte's outlook was finally not so very different from that of Rousseau.

THE AGE OF IDEOLOGY

In the 19th century there was a reaction against the attempts to explain knowledge in the abstract terms of the rationalists and empiricists of the 17th and 18th centuries. The great metaphysical systems remained, however, and, in fact, triumphed over reason in the form of "idealism." Philosophy was closely linked with the political and social upheavals of the age, and philosophers returned to considerations of how men should live.

Left: The funeral procession of those who died at the barricades in the Berlin revolution of 1848. German idealistic thinkers such as Fichte and Hegel, who believed that the world forms a unity, must be considered partly responsible for the desire to unify Germany, which was one of the aims of this revolution.

Kant

Immanuel Kant (1724–1804) was an inconspicuous lecturer in philosophy at the University of Königsberg in Prussia. Probably no one would ever have heard of him, if one day when he was already well past 40, he had not read Hume (p. 126). What he read acted on him like a catalyst. "Since the origin of metaphysics so far as we know its history," he wrote, "nothing has ever happened more decisive to its fate than the attack made upon it by David Hume."

Kant reacted so violently because he realized that unless Hume could be disproved, philosophy had reached a dead end. Hume had shown that the connection between cause and effect, which at first sight seems so necessary, is no more than a psychological habit. Man expects events to be linked together in the future as they have been in the past. Since this habit has no logical justification, it follows that Hume had undermined the concept of induction (p. 94), and with it the whole edifice of the new scientific knowledge. If Hume were right, Kant could have no more reason to suppose that the next time he drank a cup of coffee it would taste like coffee than to suppose that it would taste like peppermint cordial. And, more importantly, the laws of physics and astronomy were without rational foundation.

Such conclusions were obviously absurd. Hume had admitted so himself. But how could they be disproved? Year after year, Kant turned the problem over in his mind. Suddenly the answer struck him. Hume had tackled the problem the wrong way. He assumed the world exists independently of him. But Kant came to the conclusion that this independent existence was a myth. Nature must behave as it does because man *makes* it. But surely man does not make sugar sweet and sunshine warm. Kant's answer was in effect that he does. Kant thought man must possess certain innate faculties of mind

Left: Kant, who never traveled, lived all his life in Königsberg, East Prussia, and taught at Königsberg University. He lived to such an exact timetable that the other people of the town could set their watches by the time he passed them on his regular daily walk.

by virtue of which he imposes law and order on his experiences. The laws man discovers in nature are those he puts there himself. It is almost as if man created nature, subject to one important proviso. Kant believed that underlying man's experiences are unknowable "things-in-themselves" which would continue to exist even if there were no minds left. The role of the mind is to organize these things-in-themselves into forms which make its experiences intelligible. The result is nature.

Kant regarded the active but unconscious mental powers which he believed man possesses as *a priori* (from the earlier), by which he meant they exist in the mind prior to experience, although not as "ideas," since the content of ideas can come only from sensory experience. He believed that man applies these *a priori* faculties, which he also called forms of intuition and categories, to the creation of a necessary link between cause and effect, of the unity and identity of objects and of temporal and spatial relations. Kant did not believe that time and space belong to the universe in their own right. He thought that man goes around wearing temporal and spatial spectacles, which, of course, he cannot take off.

Kant regarded his work in philosophy as a Copernican revolution. Just as Copernicus substituted the sun for the earth as the center around which other bodies travel, so Kant substituted the mind for the outside world as the philosopher's starting point, thereby rendering nature truly intelligible for the first time. Kant embodied his conclusions in *The Critique of Pure Reason*, one of the most important books on philosophy ever written. Its importance lies in the fact that Kant is the only philosopher who has succeeded in giving an answer to the problem Hume raised. But he did so by setting strict limits to the possibilities of human knowledge. In his later *Critique of Practical Reason*, he attempted to show that the existence of God and the immortality of the soul cannot be objects of knowledge, although belief in them is a necessary precondition of moral activity and choice.

Critik

der

reinen Vernunft

von

Immanuel Kant

Professor in Königsberg.

Riga,

verlegts Johann Friedrich Hartknoch

1781.

Above: title page of the first edition of Kant's *Critique of Pure Reason*, published in 1781.

Above: the United Nations General Assembly. Kant is an undoubted influence on this organization, as the United Nations Charter of 1946 is based on one of his essays. In his work *Towards Eternal Peace* Kant won worldwide acclaim for his brilliant advocacy of political freedom.

Kant had a curious effect on the generation which followed him. On the one hand, his concern with the problem of knowledge and his idealist solution led to his thought being developed in ways he would have disapproved heartily. On the other hand, his attempt to prove by reason that things-in-themselves are forever unknowable encouraged non-philosophers to renounce reason in favor of feeling and imagination in their search for truth.

Kant's immediate philosophic successor was Johann Fichte (1762–1814), who rejected Kant's unknowable things-in-themselves for a spiritual reality which could be known through moral experience. Fichte was not alone in arguing that if nothing can be known about a reality which lies beyond experience, there can be no valid grounds for assuming such a reality exists. His universe, therefore, was not divided as Kant's was. Fichte believed that to become truly good, man needs to transcend the self and widen the whole basis of experience until he becomes identical with the Absolute. In his *Way to the Blessed Life*, Fichte wrote, "He who still has a self—in him assuredly there is nothing good." But Fichte was more of a preacher than a philosopher. His *Addresses to the German Nation* (1807–8) were intended to rouse the Germans to resist Napoleon after the battle of Jena. These addresses formed the theoretical foundation of German nationalism.

Friedrich Wilhelm Schelling (1775–1854) also abandoned Kant's things-in-themselves, but unlike Fichte he made aesthetic rather than moral experience the key to reality. He said, "The creative impulse, without intelligence, is nature; with in-

In this painting by William Blake, Newton is depicted as representing the supposed enemies of imagination—philosophy and science. The romantic thinkers believed that reality could not be found by reason and science, but only through the use of feeling and imagination.

Above: Johann Fichte (1762–1814), one of the German idealists influenced by Kant. Fichte's main work, *The Science of Knowledge*, defines philosophy as "the science of sciences," by which he means that, while the separate sciences are each devoted to only a localized subject, philosophy concerns itself with all knowledge.

Below: Friedrich Schelling (1775–1854) believed that reality was knowable. It was a form of spirit or idea, a system of reason. For him it consisted of a unity between the objective (nature) and the subjective (spirit). German idealists were trained as theologians and yearned after *certainty* about the nature of the universe.

telligence, is art." Schelling believed that spirit and nature exist separately, but as two aspects of one ultimate reality. He had a dynamic picture of God "making himself" as a spiritual being and thereby becoming involved with suffering. Schelling's early thought was pantheistic. He identified God with the universe and never entirely repudiated this view.

Friedrich Schleiermacher (1768–1834) tried to construct a transcendental philosophy of religion. He denied that religion can be intellectual, because intellectual concepts are finite and clear-cut. Similarly, religion cannot be moral, for morality, like reason, applies to the here and now. Moreover, both reason and morality apply to the space-time world. Religion is something indefinite and universal and as such can only be apprehended by intuition. In the feeling of dependence, for example, man learns of his need for God.

Fichte, Schelling and Schleiermacher all began as theological students. They were idealists who made *mind* central to their accounts of experience, and all three were influenced by Kant.

Kant's effect on the romantic movement is difficult to evaluate. He must have had some influence because he was a very eminent philosopher who claimed that reason cannot discover reality. On the other hand, the romantic movement began independently of philosophy, as a revolt against social convention and social morality. From this it spilled over into both literature and philosophy.

Fichte, Schelling and Schleiermacher all introduced an element of passion into philosophy. They lacked the calm intellectual detachment of the earlier 18th-century philosophers. Theirs was the age of the romantic poets, and there was a tendency among philosophers as well to move away from the coldness of science toward the warmth of poetry. This was always balanced, however, by the positivist admiration for science, exemplified in the philosophy of August Comte (p. 129). These two strands are reflected in contemporary schools of philosophic thought. Existentialism (p. 154) emphasizes feeling and personality, while logical empiricism (p. 152) emphasizes science.

Hegel and Marx

Above: Karl Marx's grave in Highgate cemetery, London. Marx was actively involved in the 1848 revolution in Germany; in 1849 he was exiled by the Prussian government and took refuge in London. He remained there, except for short trips, living in poverty but continuing with his studies and writing until his death in 1883.

Georg Hegel (1770–1831), the greatest speculative thinker of the 19th century, conceived of the universe as one great spiritual whole, of which man and the rest of creation are evolving parts. He thought that nothing exists, in the final analysis, but mind. He was therefore an idealist. Unlike Bishop Berkeley (p. 124), who thought that the world is an idea in the mind of God, Hegel thought the universe, which he called Absolute Mind, is identical with God. Then how could he also say it has evolving parts?

Hegel's answer was that because man is only part of the universe, he misperceives it. From man's limited viewpoint on earth, the universe certainly seems to have parts and to be evolving. If he could perceive things from the point of view of the Absolute, however, he would realize that his present opinions are largely false. Hegel believed that there are various degrees, or levels, of truth and reality, and that the more evolved anything is, the truer and more real it is. From the exalted viewpoint of the universe itself, there is no such thing as evolution. Nor are there any such entities as space and time. Man's mistaken ideas arise from his limited view.

Hegel (1770–1831) in his study. He has been regarded by some as one of the world's greatest idealistic "system-builders," and by others as a gigantic fraud. What is certain is that his influence, immense until the turn of the century, has declined greatly now. A Protestant and a Prussian, given to mystical experiences in his youth, Hegel was a professor in Berlin from 1818 until his death.

The next problem for Hegel was to explain how the process which man thinks of as historical change can occur. His theory of change is called the Dialectic. According to this theory, all change results from the clash of opposing forces, which then join to form new wholes. The first force, called the thesis, which might be anything from an idea in a mind to a natural event, contains hidden within itself the germ of its opposite, the antithesis. When the antithesis has sufficiently developed, it will challenge the thesis. The two forces are evenly matched, so neither can overcome the other, and they combine to create the synthesis. The synthesis represents a new thesis at a more evolved stage. The process then repeats itself. Steadily, however, the number of pairs becomes fewer as the oppositions that existed beneath them become absorbed. Eventually there is only one pair left. Their fusion results in the Absolute, where evolution stops.

The Hegelian conception of the universe as an evolving, dynamic, spiritual whole was very influential in the universities of Britain and the United States towards the end of the 19th century. Both the English philosopher F. H. Bradley (1846–1924) and the American Josiah Royce (1855–1916), for example, were influenced by Hegel. But the man whose interpretation and adaptation of Hegel's ideas had the greatest historical impact was Karl Marx (1818–83).

Marx became acquainted with Hegel's works while a student at the University of Berlin. From Hegel's dialectic, Marx learned that contradictions are the root of all movement, the root of all life. Like Hegel, he applied the dialectic to history. But unlike Hegel, Marx took classes instead of nations as history's units. His *Communist Manifesto* of 1848 begins, "The history of all hitherto existing society is the history of class struggle." By this Marx meant that with the exception of an original primitive communist society, there has always been a ruling class and a class which it oppresses or exploits. Marx thought that the capitalists were growing ever fatter and richer at the expense of the downtrodden army of workers. Eventually the workers would rebel and destroy the capitalists (bourgeoisie). Then, after a period of transition which Marx called the Dictatorship of the Proletariat, a classless society would arise in which the state, in the words of his collaborator Friedrich Engels (1820–95), would have "withered away."

In addition to having a different view of what constituted the units of history, Marx also differed from Hegel in his view of the fundamental nature of the universe. Hegel was an idealist, who believed that the ultimate stuff of the universe is mind or spirit. Marx was a materialist, who believed that mind is derived from matter. He thought that the forces which trigger change are to be found in the physical world. More precisely, he thought they lie in changing methods of production in industry, which should lead to new social and economic relationships between men; and these should in turn lead to the emergence of new classes.

Das Kapital.

Kritik der politischen Oekonomie.

Von

Karl Marx.

Erster Band.

Buch I: Der Produktionsprocess des Kapitals.

Hamburg

Verlag von Otto Meissner.

1867

New-York: L. W. Schmidt. 24 Barclay-Street.

Above: title page of *Das Kapital*, written by Marx in the British Museum library, using the facilities supported by the very industrial and imperialistic splendor he hoped to destroy. It became the bible of Communism.

Russian workers parading in 1929. Marx's message was "Workers of the world, unite!" and Russia was the first nation to establish his "dictatorship of the proletariat" soon after the Russian Revolution of 1917.

Ethics and the Utilitarians

Ethics is a branch of philosophy which is difficult to define exactly, but basically it is concerned with the principles of morality. It studies systematically the scope and characteristics of moral principles. What is the nature of goodness and what makes a particular action right rather than wrong? Are moral qualities, like good and evil, fundamental and indefinable? Or can they always be derived from other qualities, so that the good merely means what is pleasant, or what benefits the state? What is the difference, if there is one, between happiness and pleasure? Can the will be free?

The main problem, which implicates most of the others or makes them irrelevant, is that of whether moral qualities are intrinsic or derived. The latter view is fashionable today. Goodness has come to be thought of as a "naturalistic" quality, composed of, or derived from, a complex of nonethical qualities. Nonetheless, there are difficulties about such a view, which Plato, Kant and Moore, to name only three philosophers, found overwhelming. For example, what is the meaning of a question like "Is the good that which brings satisfaction?" If the good can be explained away naturalistically, as meaning "the satisfying" or "the pleasant," substitution of this expression for "the good" makes the question meaningless. Yet the question obstinately refuses to lie down; it refuses to die. The concept of an objective right and wrong cannot be disposed of so easily after all.

Two men who were particularly concerned with what makes an action right were the Englishmen

Below: engraving showing Queen Victoria of England going to church. John Stuart Mill criticized the prudery of conventional Christianity in the Victorian era during which he lived, and argued for a simpler and more direct faith. "In the golden rule of Jesus of Nazareth we read the complete spirit of the Ethics of utility," he said. To love your neighbor as yourself is the ideal of utilitarian morality.

Above: John Stuart Mill (1806–73), educated by his father, James Mill, who shared Jeremy Bentham's utilitarian views on ethics. The younger Mill agreed mainly, but where they taught that good should be measured by the pleasure it brought, he argued for quality as well—"better Socrates dissatisfied than a pig satisfied."

Below: Bentham's design for a model prison. Bentham was a hedonist, believing the doctrine that whatever is pleasant is good. Thus the more people who could be happy, the better. He urged the revision of the penal system, on the grounds that the function of imprisonment should be to reform rather than merely to punish.

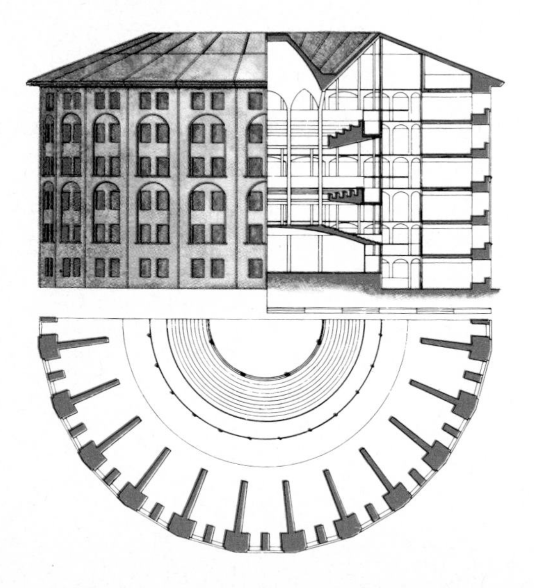

Jeremy Bentham (1748–1832) and John Stuart Mill (1806–73). Both came to the same conclusion, that the right action in a given set of circumstances is the one which has the best consequences—a view which became known as utilitarianism. They further decided that the best consequences are those which produce the greatest sum of happiness, or balance of happiness over unhappiness, for everyone affected by the action, although each of them interpreted this theory in a slightly different way.

Jeremy Bentham became interested in ethics and politics through studying law; the aim of legislation, in his view, should be to arrange rewards and punishments so that everyone, in pursuing his own interests, will in fact increase the general welfare even though that is not his purpose. He thought that the good is pleasure and nothing else (a view known as "ethical hedonism"), and defined the greatest good as a state of affairs in which there is the greatest possible balance of pleasure over pain. Pleasure he equated with happiness, so that for him the good, the pleasant and the happy were synonymous terms. However, the ordinary person makes a sharp distinction between the good and the pleasant, and if asked, would say that whereas they sometimes coincide, they often do not. Any philosophy which denies the distinction between them must be prepared to give a convincing explanation of how the apparent distinction arose.

John Stuart Mill was brought up by his father, James Mill, on Bentham's principles. He dreamed of a society which would have "the greatest happiness of the greatest number," but found it difficult to work out what this would mean in practice. Mill tried to distinguish between different kinds of pleasure, because he was afraid that otherwise people would interpret his teaching as a rationale for indulging in their favorite vices. Here, of course, he ran into a logical difficulty. How could he persuade people that the pleasures of the mind, for example, were preferable to those of the body if they did not believe him? Only by reference to some sort of moral standard other than pleasure. But this was precisely what his own philosophy forbade.

Anti-Rationalists

Arthur Schopenhauer, Sören Kierkegaard and Friedrich Nietzsche stood in stark opposition to the academic trends of their day. While Schopenhauer and Nietzsche argued that the important thing in life is the will rather than reason, Kierkegaard stressed the importance of feeling and faith. All three philosophers united in denouncing the prevailing Hegelianism. It is safe, therefore, to call them anti-rationalists.

Schopenhauer (1788–1860) was a curious mixture of a man, combining interest in the religions of the East with admiration for Kant, and extreme pessimism with a belief in the omnipotent power of the will. He rarely used the term *will* in the same sense twice, however. Sometimes he seemed to regard it as energy, sometimes as an instinctive drive, sometimes as a blind striving and sometimes as the human will to live; but never as our conscious wishes and purposes. One thing he was sure of—the result was always evil. The world was full of illusion, sorrow and strife. Nor did he believe any paradise awaited man, as Christians thought.

Schopenhauer's theory that the will possessed its

Above left: Schopenhauer was influenced in his conception of the world as a unity and in his belief in the limitations of reason by the Indian philosophy of the Upanishads, as well as by Kant. He said, "Reason is feminine by nature. It can only give after it has received." Knowledge, he believed, depended not on reason but on will. To know reality, he held, we must look inward and then we see ourselves as willing. When we act, we extend or realize the goals of the will. Left: whereas Schopenhauer had introduced the notion of will to augment that of reason, the Danish philosopher, Kierkegaard, developed the notion of feeling. Dread and anxiety make us aware of being. Through our feelings of guilt and remorse we gain knowledge of morality and the freedom of will, he believed. Though of little influence in his time, Kierkegaard is now regarded as the first existentialist. It was 100 years before his ideas became well known.

Right: a German cartoon of 1905 showing a churchgoer "protecting his family against the spectacle of nudity." Both Schopenhauer and Nietzsche rejected Christianity and its prudery. Kierkegaard did not.

own cunning, which enabled it to achieve its desires, parallels the theory of a vital force *(élan vital)* held by the French philosopher Henri Bergson (1859–1941). Bergson believed that this force is responsible for evolution. He regarded life as a constant flow or surging wave, which is constantly cut up by the intellect into separate bits. It is the *élan vital* which gives this flow its motive force.

Both Schopenhauer and Bergson, therefore, had what might be called an immanent view of evolution as an inner force. Their opinions contrast with the scientific theory of evolution put forward by Darwin. According to his theory of natural selection, those species survive which by chance happen to develop variations which suit their physical and organic environment.

Kierkegaard (1813–55) is generally regarded as the first existentialist. He rebelled not only against the "system" of Hegel, but also against the whole conception of timeless, changeless values which had entered the bloodstream of European thought through Plato and the Greeks. Kierkegaard thought morality should concern itself with crisis situations where rules and universal principles offer no guidance, and he held that faith, rather than reason, provided the key to life. He argued subtly and often wittily that a reasonable faith was useless; faith is the acceptance of paradox, and requires a "leap" beyond reason.

The German philosopher, Friedrich Nietzsche, whose most important writings include *Thus Spake Zarathustra* and *Beyond Good and Evil.*

The philosophy of Nietzsche (1844–1900) is also important as an early form of existentialism. He begins with the premise that God is dead. Man must therefore take upon himself the burden of knowledge and moral responsibility. Nietzsche was not advocating undisciplined license, however. He admired strength of will and thought that man needs to exercise stringent self-discipline. Nietzsche called himself an "immoralist" in the sense that he rejected any concept of an underlying moral code, which he believed leads only to complacency or conformity. Any "code" must be one which fits the individual and enables him to live with himself, rather than one to which the individual chains himself.

In this context, Nietzsche criticized Christianity (although he admired Jesus) and other religious orthodoxies as growing out of, and perpetuating, despair. He thought men basically are continually striving to achieve a higher level of being, to overcome their passions and be creative rather than simply creatures of their world. This higher being Nietzsche called the overman or superman; and while perhaps no one has ever reached this level, he did not think men should be circumscribed by moralities or values imposed by those too weak to attempt the struggle.

C. S. Peirce (1839–1914), probably the first pragmatist, said that all true statements must have practical consequences. A trained chemist and mathematican, he was also a very original logician. He judged his discoveries in logic to be his most important work.

Pragmatism differs from the empirical movement founded by Locke (p. 123) in that it stresses the active, constructive role of the mind in experience. Following in Locke's footsteps, British empiricists have always tended to see the mind as passive in perception. From Locke to Russell, they have made a rigid distinction between the mind which knows and the object known. Also, most of them have regarded experience as composed of distinct sensations, between which the mind interposes links.

American pragmatists would have none of this. How absurd, thought William James (1842–1910), to base a theory of perception on the view that experience reaches us in separate pieces. "Consciousness does not appear to itself chopped up in bits," he said. Pragmatists think that experiences arrive as a stream of conscious life which the mind then breaks up into objects, relationships and so forth. Heraclitus and Bergson (p. 84, 141) thought this too. The distinguishing feature of pragmatic thought is the emphasis it places on the *way* in which the flow of experience is broken up by the mind; for pragmatists the flow is always broken up in a manner which serves a purpose in human needs for active manipulation of the world.

This emphasis on action stems from the basic pragmatic belief that thinking is a biological response by living organisms to their environment. There is thus a great sympathy with science, especially biology, at the heart of pragmatism. Yet pragmatism interprets the laws of science in its own special way. Indeed, it does not regard them as laws in the accepted sense at all. Rather, laws are hypotheses or postulates which can be discarded if the consequences of believing them are unsatisfactory.

There is undoubtedly something refreshing about the way that pragmatists link up thinking with life as a whole. And yet, unfortunately, pragmatism seems to go too far. It does not confine its utility principle to responses of organisms to difficult situations in life, but seeks to apply it to conceptual problems, even in logic and mathematics. Indeed, it sometimes even tries to use the principle as a test of truth.

"The 'true,'" said James, "to put it very briefly, is only the expedient in our way of thinking, just as the 'right' is only the expedient in our way of behaving." This makes practical advantage the test of truth instead of correspondence with fact, a belief which if taken literally has curious consequences. James thought that one had a right to religious or

The French philosopher Henri Bergson (1859–1941) believed that reality was a continuous, evolving stream of activity. According to him the intellect misrepresents time as a succession of distinct separate units, rather as the high-speed photographs below have frozen the successive motions of the galloping horse. In actual fact the horse's movements are continuous, and, similarly, time is continuous.

other beliefs if they were personally satisfying and not contradicted by available evidence. But this implies that completely opposing beliefs, for example theism and atheism, can both be "true."

The founder of pragmatism was the American Charles Sanders Peirce (1839–1914). He rejected determinism and sought the meanings of concepts, not in the images they called to mind, but in the practical effects of believing or applying them. Both he and the last great American pragmatist, the New Englander John Dewey (1859–1952), tried to improve on the pragmatist opinion that the true is the useful. Dewey, who had a special interest in biology, was also influenced by Hegel. He made *inquiry* the essence of logic, rather than truth and falsity. "Inquiry" was regarded by Dewey as a form of mutual adjustment between an organism and its environment. The object of adjustment was to locate and remove failures of adaptation, and to reconstitute the organism-environment relation as a whole. Dewey thought that academic philosophy was far too static. The certainty it pursued, in particular, was a will-o-the-wisp. Beliefs should be regarded as instruments which may always be improved or discarded, rather than as principles true in themselves.

Dewey was a professor of philosophy at the University of Chicago and at Columbia University. He was deeply interested in education and social reform. Through books such as *The School and Society*, which criticized the tendency of educational systems to teach the solutions of past problems rather than the ways of solving new ones, Dewey had a great influence on American education.

Above: John Dewey (1859–1952) taught philosophy at several American universities. Widely traveled, he studied methods of education in Russia, China and Japan. He had an immense influence in the United States as a theoretical and practical philosopher, but is now remembered mainly for his ideas on education and moral reform.

Above: the pragmatist philosopher William James (1842–1910), on the right, with his brother Henry, the novelist. William was a physiologist and psychologist as well as a philosopher, and used the empirical methods of biology to seek physiological bases for behavior and mental activities. He taught mainly at Harvard.

THE 20TH-CENTURY REVOLUTION

In the 20th century, the division which began to appear in the 19th century has become wider. On the one hand, existentialists consider the importance of man's life as a whole. On the other hand, and primarily in the Anglo-Saxon world, there is an analytic emphasis. These philosophers are concerned with analyzing meaning and language. There have been signs of a synthesis of analytic methods and interest in the whole range of human activity, but whether or not it will be achieved remains to be seen.

Composition (1954), by Victor Vasarely. This typifies the trend among modern abstract artists to give visual expression both to a personal approach and to a strictly analytic approach. Such a combination, however, is lacking in most modern philosophy, where the different schools of thought appear to be moving in directions that are opposite and irreconcilable.

Whitehead

Alfred North Whitehead (1861–1947) was an Englishman who specialized in mathematics before going to teach philosophy at Harvard in 1924. His most important work, *Process and Reality*, developed what he called a "philosophy of organism," which attempts a vast synthesis of philosophy and science. The object of Whitehead's work was to present a view of the cosmos which avoids equating abstractions with reality—a tendency which Whitehead found too frequent in modern science.

He considered, for example, the scientific analysis of nature. According to the scientist, there is no light or color in nature. These so-called secondary qualities are contributed by man. In attacking this view, Whitehead wrote, "Thus nature gets credit which should in truth be reserved for ourselves: the rose for its scent: the nightingale for his song: and the sun for its radiance. They should address their lyrics to themselves, and should turn them into odes of self-congratulation on the excellence of the human mind. Nature is a dull affair, soundless, scentless, colorless; merely the hurrying of material, endlessly, meaninglessly."

Whitehead did not mean to infer even obliquely that physics has no value. What he did mean to suggest was that it does not tell the whole story. There is more to a pretty face than electrons in motion. The physicist, too, would admit this, but he is too prone to suggest that the face is somehow derived from the electrons, with the added implication that this makes the electrons more relevant than the face in explaining the world. It is these ideas that Whitehead attacked.

Whitehead denied that the world's religious and artistic movements, and the humanities in general, are merely the offshoots or by-products of the world of nature that has been discovered by physics. On

Left: the English metaphysician Alfred N. Whitehead (1861–1947). After *Principia Mathematica*, written with Russell, Whitehead's interest moved gradually to metaphysics. He believed that the perceiver was an interacting part of the nature he perceived, and that events or occasions are short-lived pulses of feeling or experience. Thus a botanist will look at poppies (below) in a different way from an artist (below right), yet both perceive poppies.

the contrary, if any world has to be rejected, it must be the world of science. For the scientist has failed to realize that what he has discovered is only a collection of abstractions. They are very useful, to be sure, in their practical applications—for example, the discovery of electric light, guns and so forth—but they are not to be equated with the underlying "stuff" of the world.

Whitehead thought that many of the "problems" of philosophy and science spring from the split made between mind and matter, beginning with Descartes (p. 118) in the 17th century. Whitehead denied that there is any such distinction. He postulated a single stuff or process, every part of which interacts with every other part. His view of the universe was thus somewhat similar to that of Hegel (p. 136).

The essence of Whitehead's stuff or process, which is neither mind nor matter, seems to be something akin to feeling. Things "take note of" each other. "Eternal objects," somewhat like Plato's forms, penetrate the world of spatiotemporal events because of the activity of God. But the analogy with Plato must not be pressed too closely for, apart from the spatiotemporal flux, the eternal objects themselves are only abstractions.

Whitehead believed God is the principle of actuality and limitation. He is the principle of actuality because he determines the existing world by allowing the manifestation of particular eternal objects in the world. He is the principle of limitation, because he excludes all other possible worlds. No reason can be given for God himself because he is the "ground of rationality." He is beyond reason and is therefore described by Whitehead as the "Ultimate Irrationality."

Right: Whitehead (center), professor at London's Imperial College of Science and Technology (1914–1924), with members of his staff. While there, he wrote *Enquiries Concerning the Principles of Natural Knowledge, The Concept of Nature* and *The Principle of Relativity*. In 1924 he left to join the department of philosophy at Harvard.

Right: a page from Russell and Whitehead's *Principia Mathematica* (1910–13), showing the notation they used in their mathematical logic. In this work, logic and mathematics merge into one system, derived from a new elementary logic which Russell called the "propositional calculus." It was a crucial philosophic discovery.

348 PROLEGOMENA TO CARDINAL ARITHMETIC [PART II

∗52·01. $1 = \hat{\alpha}\{(\exists x) . \alpha = \iota‘x\}$ Df

∗52·1. $\vdash : \alpha \epsilon 1 . \equiv . (\exists x) . \alpha = \iota‘x$ [∗20·3 . (∗52·01)]

∗52·11. $\vdash :. \alpha \epsilon 1 . \equiv : (\exists x) : y \epsilon \alpha . \equiv_y . y = x$ [∗52·1 . ∗51·14]

∗52·12. $\vdash : \hat{z}(\phi z) \epsilon 1 . \equiv . E!(\imath x)(\phi x)$

Dem.

$\vdash . ∗52·11 . \supset \vdash :. \hat{z}(\phi z) \epsilon 1 . \equiv : (\exists x) : y \epsilon \hat{z}(\phi z) . \equiv_y . y = x :$

[∗20·3] $\equiv : (\exists x) : \phi y . \equiv_y . y = x :$

[∗14·11] $\equiv : E!(\imath x)(\phi x) :. \supset \vdash .$ Prop

∗52·13. $\vdash . 1 = D‘\iota$

Dem.

$\vdash . ∗51·131 . \supset \vdash : \alpha = \iota‘x . \equiv . \alpha \iota x :$

[∗10·11·281] $\supset \vdash : (\exists x) . \alpha = \iota‘x . \equiv . (\exists x) . \alpha \iota x :$

[∗52·1] $\supset \vdash : \alpha \epsilon 1 . \equiv . (\exists x) . \alpha \iota x$

[∗33·13] $\equiv . \alpha \epsilon D‘\iota : \supset \vdash .$ Prop

∗52·14. $\vdash . 1 = \iota“V$ [∗52·13 . ∗37·28]

∗52·15. $\vdash : \alpha \epsilon 1 . \equiv . E! \breve{\iota}‘\alpha$ [∗51·54 . ∗52·1]

∗52·16. $\vdash :. \alpha \epsilon 1 . \equiv : \exists ! \alpha : x, y \epsilon \alpha . \supset_{x,y} . x = y$ [∗52·15 . ∗51·55 . ∗14·203]

The philosophy of Bertrand Russell (born 1872) spans a period of nearly 70 years, from the turn of the century almost to the present day. Throughout this period Russell has striven to provide a new logical basis for philosophy and to clear up the metaphysical clutter left over from the past.

Russell continues the British empirical tradition which dates back to Locke and Hume. While Locke and Hume believed that philosophers should analyze ideas, and as a result indulged in a psychological analysis of the mind's contents, Russell's opinion has been that the object of philosophical analysis should be the proposition. Propositions, unlike ideas, are true or false. They are the *objects* of ideas and remarks, rather than the ideas or remarks themselves.

By making propositions instead of ideas the main subject for philosophic investigation, Russell placed philosophy on a more technical and impersonal basis than before, when it had to rely on an analysis of ideas that might vary with the individual concerned. Whether Russell's dream of a partnership between philosophy and science has come true is open to doubt, but there can be no doubt as to his revitalizing influence on philosophy as a whole. He appeared at the turn of the century like St. George on his charger, using new logical techniques to slay the old metaphysical dragons whenever he could.

A good example of his method is his celebrated "theory of descriptions," which attempts to solve the problem of falsity. The problem, expressed briefly, is that of how it is possible to affirm that something is not the case. To take one of Russell's own examples, suppose someone says, "The golden mountain does not exist." It seems that in the very act of denying it exists, he must refer to it, and thereby attribute some sort of existence to it.

Suppose we ask, "What do you mean in your

Left: Russell's birthplace at Ravenscroft, Wales. Of Russell, Beatrice Webb said, "Intellectually he is audacious and iconoclast, detesting social or religious convention, suspecting sentiment, believing only in the order of thought and the order of things, in logic and in science."

Three 19th-century mathematicians who helped to put mathematics on a purely logical, nonempirical basis: George Boole (left), who presented a new nonquantitative algebra of formal logic; Bernhard Riemann (center), whose "elliptic" geometry, in which parallel lines do not meet, took geometry beyond the familiar spatial relationships; and Gottlob Frege (right), whose attempt to derive mathematics from logic anticipated that of Whitehead and Russell.

statement by 'the golden mountain?'" He can reply either that he means an imaginary mountain or a real one. The first reply is not to the point; he is not trying to assert that imaginary golden mountains do not exist, but that real ones do not. This throws him back to the second alternative, which means that we can paraphrase his original remark by saying, "The real golden mountain does not exist"—an obvious contradiction. It is a problem that has troubled philosophers since the time of the Greeks.

Russell's solution is to rephrase the offending statement, "the golden mountain does not exist," in such a way that the expression "the golden mountain" disappears. In his *History of Western Philosophy*, he rephrases it as follows: "There is no entity C such that 'X is golden and mountainous' is true when X is C, but not otherwise." It is not really necessary to grasp the algebra involved here to appreciate what Russell has done. He has removed the descriptive expression, "the golden mountain," which tricked us into regarding it as a symbol complete in itself. With its removal goes the temptation to invent a metaphysical problem.

In addition to being a philosopher, Russell was a brilliant mathematician. With Alfred North Whitehead, his former teacher, he wrote *Principia Mathematica* (three volumes, 1910–13). They believed that mathematics and logic are the same, and that the entire body of pure mathematics can be constructed from logical axioms.

Throughout his life, Russell has also shown a passionate interest in freedom. He has been a pacifist, and his views, particularly on issues concerning the United States and Russia, have often made him a focal point of controversy in the West.

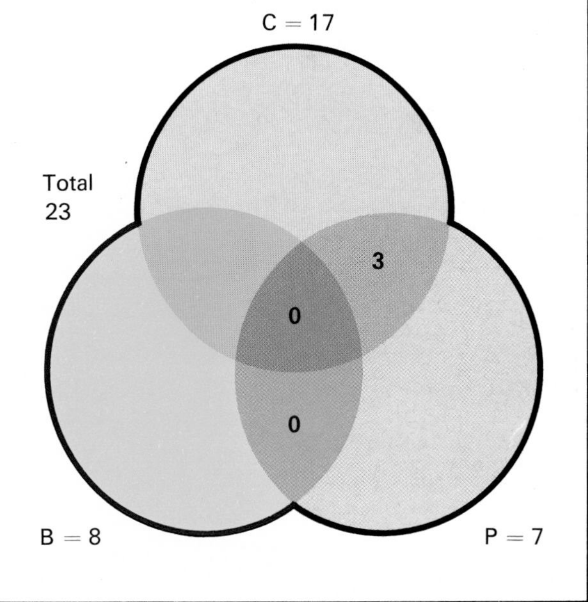

The Mathematical Analysis of Logic, by the Englishman George Boole, was published in 1847. In this work Boole treated the laws of Aristotle's logic in a new algebraic way. Later, the mathematician John Venn (1834–1923) used diagrammatic methods to explain the complex notation of Boole's system of symbolic logic. Above is a typical problem treated in this way.

G. E. Moore

The British philosopher, George Edward Moore, attacked subjectivist views in ethics in his *Principia Ethica*. To understand Moore's philosophic views it is necessary to over-simplify those views slightly and say that Moore rejected the egotistical claim made by the subjectivists that beauty not only lay in the eye of the beholder but that it had a right to lie there. In his opinion, the mere fact that most people would describe the view on the right as gentle and the view immediately below as harsh does not make those judgments correct, but merely popular.

Moore's beliefs can be extended and better understood if you compare two such different views as these pictures of exactly the same liner (above and left). Moore supported the Platonic belief that such differing views of the same object may produce differing reactions in the senses, or even in the more inward realm of understanding. He went on to say that the analytic method of science could be applied to both our physical and mental worlds. Objects of thought, values and ideas have, he claimed, an objective existence. Individual minds can perceive and know these ideas but they do not influence these abstract and independent truths.

The original logical empiricists were a group of philosophers and mathematicians who formed around Moritz Schlick (1882–1936) in Vienna in the early 1920s. The group was known as the Vienna Circle and as the logical positivists; however, they preferred to call themselves logical empiricists.

The logical empiricists disliked traditional philosophy and wished to find it a new, useful task to perform. They therefore had to begin by finding a way of ruling out metaphysics, and then decide what philosophy was going to do instead. To understand how they approached these tasks, it is first necessary to grasp the difference between two kinds of statement..

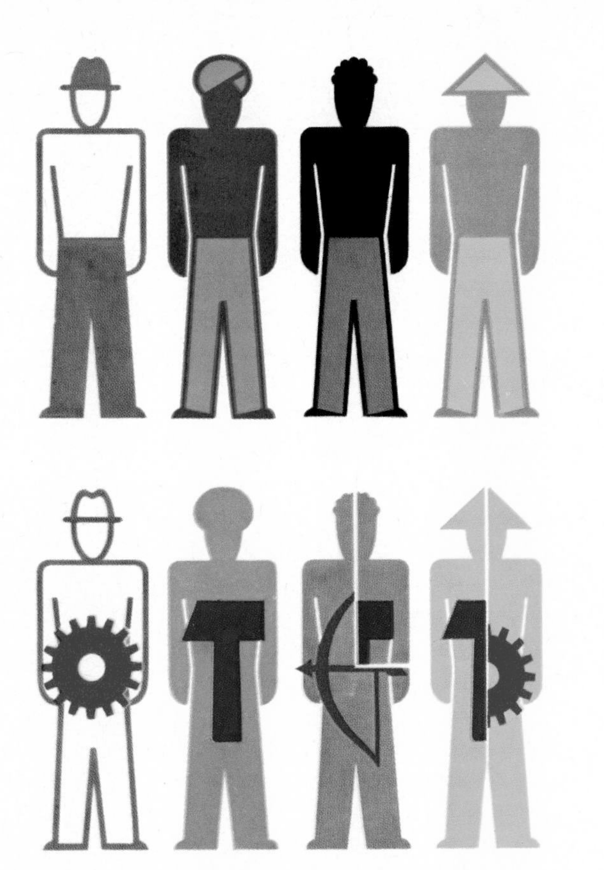

Above: an example of the use of the international picture language developed by Otto Neurath (1882–1945), the Austrian logical empiricist who was one of the Vienna Circle. Using symbols called "isotypes," it was designed to solve problems of communication in education. The logical empiricists believed that the function of philosophy is to clarify and standardize the structure of language and Neurath established his Isotype Institute for this purpuse.

There are statements made about the world, whether scientific or general, and statements or propositions of logic and mathematics. The first are called empirical. They are also called contingent, which means that any fact about the world might have been different. The propositions of logic and mathematics are called necessary or *a priori,* to signify that it is impossible to imagine them different without a contradiction. They are true or false by virtue of their meaning alone.

An example will bring out the distinction between the two sorts of statement. If a man says, "There goes George" as George passes by, it is possible to imagine that Harry might have been passing by instead, or that no one might have been passing by at all. If someone remarks that two and two make four, it is impossible to imagine the remark false without a contradiction. This difference between the empirical and the *a priori* had been recognized by philosophers for centuries, but the logical empiricists used it in a special way. They claimed that no statement can be significant or meaningful unless it belongs to one of these two classes. To which class, then, do metaphysical propositions such as "God exists" belong? They are not logical or mathematical. Might they be empirical?

Here the logical empiricists introduced a new idea. They declared that empirical remarks (remarks about the world) can only be significant if it is possible, at least in theory, to confirm or refute them by specific sensory experiences. If no conceivable empirical test is relevant to a remark's truth or falsity, it follows that the remark is meaningless. Value judgments of morality and art are also empirically meaningless by this test, although they can be regarded as expressions of approval and disapproval rather than as assertions.

This test for the intelligibility of remarks about

Right: one of the hundreds of units (actual size) for logic circuitry used in the FX-1 computer at the Massachusetts Institute of Technology. To analyze the data fed into it, the computer is programmed with the same rules of logic as those used by the logical empiricists in their analysis of the meanings of propositions.

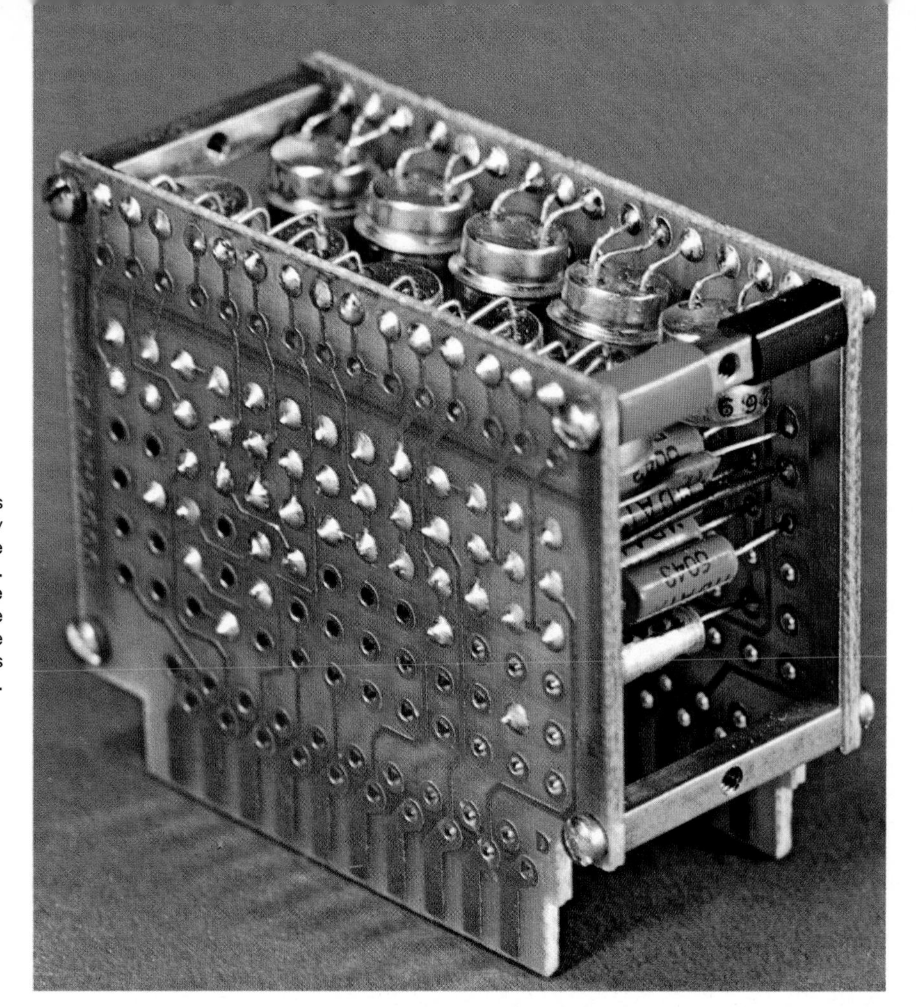

the world was called the "verification principle." There were difficulties in applying it to statements about the past, but it did rule out metaphysics. Suppose someone reading Bishop Berkeley (p. 124) declared that the physical book in which he was learning the Bishop's opinions existed only in his mind. Since no possible empirical test could prove him right or wrong, it would follow that his claim was meaningless.

Logical empiricists were quite prepared to admit that language can be used in nonfactual ways; and that moral, aesthetic and metaphysical judgments might have nonfactual uses. The latter might produce an attitude toward life akin to that of the poet, for example. But they would not then be statements about philosophy.

The constructive work of philosophy continues. Philosophy is conceived of by many philosophers today as analysis, the task of the analyst being to clear up ambiguities and to clarify the meanings of statements. In this view, philosophical inquiry does not result in new or revised knowledge about the world, but it reveals more clearly the meanings of the propositions made about it.

The original logical empiricists were a group of Austrian philosophers, mathematicians and scientists who called themselves the Vienna Circle. Their first leader was Moritz Schlick (right), then a professor at Berlin, who was killed in 1936. Because of the hostile political climate of the Nazi regime, the other members left Austria. One of them, Rudolf Carnap (left), brought the group's ideas to the United States when he established himself there.

Existentialism

The modern European philosophies which have been grouped together under the name of existentialism are all philosophies of protest against theoretical and scientific thought. There have always been philosophies of this nature, but none of them is regarded as existentialist before Kierkegaard (p. 140). What distinguishes the existentialist from his forebears is not so much his repudiation of existing creeds as his strident individualism, his strangely personal note of anguish, his lack of romanticism and his preoccupation with death, fear, alienation, self-awareness and guilt. Above all, there is his feeling that man's existence is something unique which he has to live through rather than understand objectively and impersonally.

There is, however, no single positive belief which existentialists share. Indeed, when the two most famous existentialists of the last 40 years, Karl Jaspers and Martin Heidegger, heard that Jean Paul Sartre said that he was an existentialist, they immediately said they were not, so that no one would think they shared the same interests as Sartre.

Heidegger (born 1889) and Jaspers (born 1883) are very difficult to summarize and in places their writings are very obscure. Heidegger was influenced by Edmund Husserl (1859–1938), the founder of a philosophical school of thought called phenomenology. Husserl thought that man's perceptions about the world are based on intuitive experiences. Therefore, in order to have any understanding of the natural world, philosophers should concentrate not, in fact, on the natural world itself but on man's inner experiences.

Heidegger makes a general attack on logic and science. He is tormented by a vision of death, which will eventually render all man's efforts futile. He emphasizes that man feels abandoned and incomplete in a world he did not make, but that recognition of his isolation and incompleteness is the necessary clue to authentic self-understanding.

Jaspers thinks that philosophy can begin only when reason has "suffered shipwreck." Although he criticizes Nietzsche, he also praises him, together with Kierkegaard, as the only original philosophers of their age, because their thinking derived from personal experience rather than academic schools. Jaspers believes in a state of being he calls "transcendence," which is beyond our knowledge. But he says neither the scriptures nor philosophy can teach man how to live.

Sartre (born 1905) has written a number of novels and plays as well as philosophical works and is, on the whole, easier to understand than his German

A scene from the film *Les Mains Sales*, from a work by Jean Paul Sartre. Sartre is the best-known exponent of the existentialist movement which, in France, has very close associations with literature. As well as his philosophical treatise, *Being and Nothingness*, Sartre has written several novels. His heroes are outside society, without links to tradition or convention. Alone, they choose their own destiny.

Above: the German existentialist Karl Jaspers. This quotation from his *Existenphilosophie* summarizes his ideas: "The individual cannot become human by himself. Self-being is only real in communion with another self-being. Alone, I sink into gloomy isolation. . . ."

Above: a French Resistance poster. Sartre, the French existentialist, fought in the Resistance during the German occupation. His writings show a vivid psychological insight into problems connected with fear, death, decision and responsibility, which he encountered at first-hand during these years of turmoil in France.

contemporaries. His starting point is a distinction between the unconscious thing that exists "in itself" *(en-soi)* and the conscious being who exists "for itself" *(pour-soi)*. Man is unique in having self-awareness, which the rest of the world lacks. A table is what it is, and that is that. But linked with man's self-awareness is the possibility of choice. A man is not a lawyer in the same way that he is tall or old. He has to choose his career, whereas he cannot choose his age.

This freedom, together with the immense responsibility it entails, brings anxiety in its train. Since Sartre is an atheist, he believes that man must make his own values in a world without God. He is forced to be free and to make decisions, and therein lies his tragic absurdity. In analyzing how man reacts to this situation, Sartre deals with man's tendency to deceive himself. He tries to escape the anxiety of recognizing his freedom and responsibility, for example, by refusing to admit that he has to make decisions for as long as possible and by living in a conformist, routine way. He is insincere in his relationships with other people.

Sartre has also struggled consistently to make existentialism compatible with Marxism. Interestingly, some Marxists have criticized existentialism as the capitalists' philosophy of despair, resulting from their inability to prevent wars.

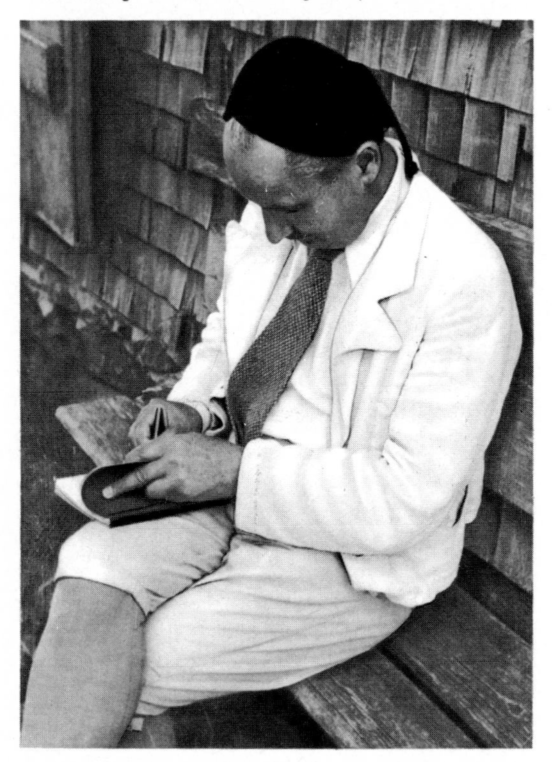

Above: German philosopher, Martin Heidegger, who, with Sartre, holds that man is unique because he determines his own existence. Like Hegel, Heidegger glorified the state and so became a supporter of the Nazis.

Wittgenstein

Ludwig Wittgenstein (1889–1951), who was born in Vienna, studied engineering in Berlin and philosophy at Cambridge, England, before joining the Austrian army in World War I. Taken prisoner by the Italians, he proceeded to write the *Tractatus Logico-Philosophicus*, his only work published during his lifetime. This book reflects Russell's (p. 148) influence and had a profound effect on the various schools of logical empiricism (p. 152) and linguistic analysis that were then springing up. Wittgenstein wrote that language expresses a picture of reality by means of propositions. A proposition which pictures a possible fact is meaningful; one which pictures an actual fact is true. Statements of logic and mathematics are true by virtue of their form or symbols alone. Metaphysical statements, Wittgenstein said, are meaningless. The object of philosophy should be "the logical clarification of thought."

Eventually Wittgenstein began to doubt the views he expressed in the *Tractatus*, and after some years he repudiated them entirely. He retained the problem of language as central to philosophy, and his conviction that metaphysics is impossible; but in every other respect his thought underwent a great change. He no longer thought there is any general form which all propositions share. On the contrary, language has a great variety of forms, which often overlap. The reason philosophic problems arise is that both philosophers and nonphilosophers misunderstand the relationship between language and life. They try to divorce words from their ordinary meanings and give them special philosophic ones. If people remembered that language is an instrument of life and must be used as such, philosophic "problems" would cease to trouble them, for these arise not when language is "doing work," but when it is "like an engine idling."

Then what were the old philosophers doing when they tried to discover the real nature of the self, free will, the good, physical objects and so on, and wondered whether these things existed? And what were the early 20th-century philosophers doing when they asked the same sorts of questions about propositions? Did they really mean to claim that they did not know what these various concepts meant? They certainly knew how to *use* them.

Wittgenstein uses the concept of understanding to illustrate his meaning. Philosophers have searched for the meaning of this concept as if understanding were a special kind of mental event that occurs in people's heads. If they considered the word's *use*, they would realize it is nothing of the kind. When someone says he understands, it is simply not true that the understanding must occur in him in some kind of flash. On the contrary, the test of whether he has understood will be whether he reacts the right way when the occasion demands. That is why Wittgenstein says that the meaning is the use.

To illustrate the mistake philosophers make, Wittgenstein likens words to the pieces used in a game. The meaning of a word, he then says, is its role in the game. The philosopher who is baffled by the meaning of the word "understanding" becomes like a man who wants to learn the meaning of the pawn in chess—but stipulates that this meaning must be something different from the moves which the pawn can and cannot make.

The few works which Wittgenstein wrote during the second half of his life were only published after his death, but the unique personality of the man served to make him a legend during his lifetime. His *Philosophical Investigations* is an immensely stimulating book full of actual examples of analysis which provoke the reader to think for himself.

4·3 The truth-possibilities of the elementary propositions mean the possibilities of the existence and non-existence of the atomic facts.

4·31 The truth-possibilities can be presented by schemata of the following kind ("T" means "true", "F" "false". The rows of T's and F's under the row of the elementary propositions mean their truth-possibilities in an easily intelligible symbolism).

p	q	r
T	T	T
F	T	T
T	F	T
T	T	F
F	F	T
F	T	F
T	F	F
F	F	F

p	q
T	T
F	T
T	F
F	F

p
T
F

In his *Tractatus Logico-Philosophicus*, Wittgenstein maintained that philosophy was, essentially, the process of clarification. The "truth table" above is his attempt to reduce all statements to their simplest elements that cannot be broken down any further.

Above: in his *Tractatus*, Wittgenstein thought it possible to have a perfect language defining everything with great precision. Later his views changed. "What is the criterion of the sameness of two images?" he asked. "Is the reflection the same as the reality? It may be to you, but someone else may see it very differently."

Below: a diagram representing the evolution of modern philosophy. The red lines linking the philosophers or their ideas indicate antagonism or reaction to each other's views, like the pragmatists rejecting Hegel and German idealism. The green lines show a positive influence—like that of Hegel on British idealism.

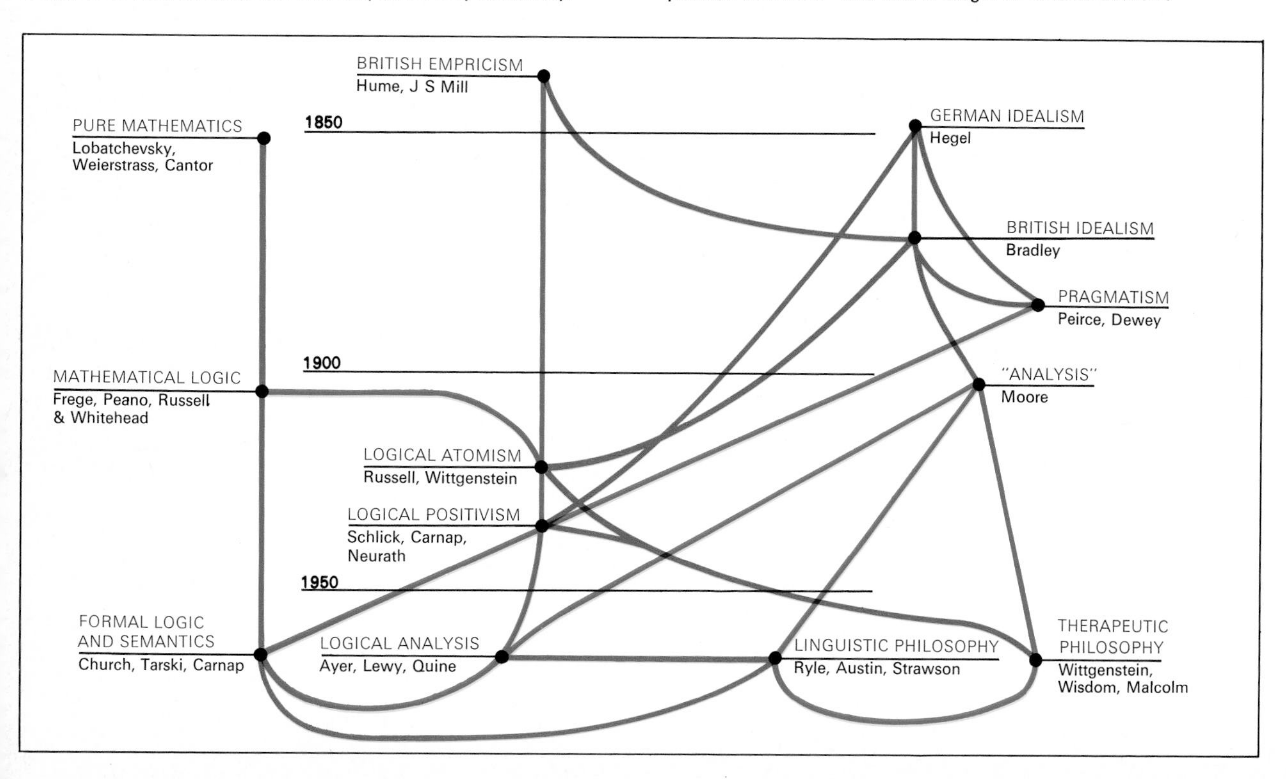

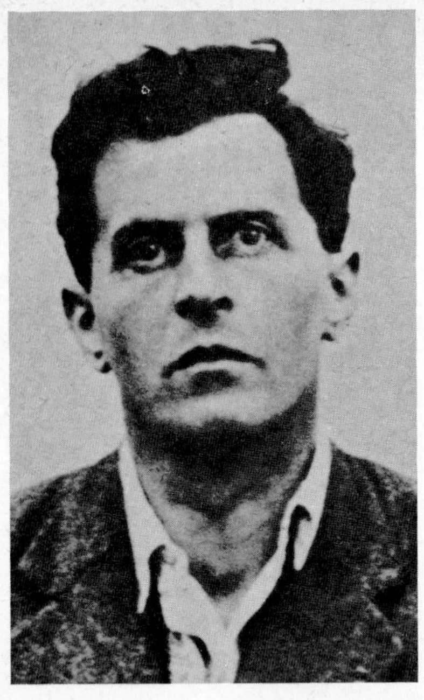

Ludwig Wittgenstein (left) was a logician who became interested in linguistic philosophy. His ideas in this field were taken from lecture notes and papers collected after his death and published in 1953 under the title *Philosophical Investigations*. Simply put, he believed that language was a system, rather like a game. The meaning of a word could vary depending on what it was used to qualify, describe or generally signify. With the use of words, as in different games, we use different sets of rules. Solitaire, the card game (below), depends on luck, not on competition. Snakes and ladders (bottom left), a British children's game, also depends on luck but adds competition. Even casual street games (bottom center) have some rules. Chess (bottom right) and roulette (right) both involve competition, but chess requires skill and roulette is a game of chance. As all games have a "family resemblance," having rules and luck or skill in common, so too with words and their meanings, according to Wittgenstein. To ask what a word means, he said, is like asking what a chess pawn is. We cannot give a precise definition—we can only explain how it is used.

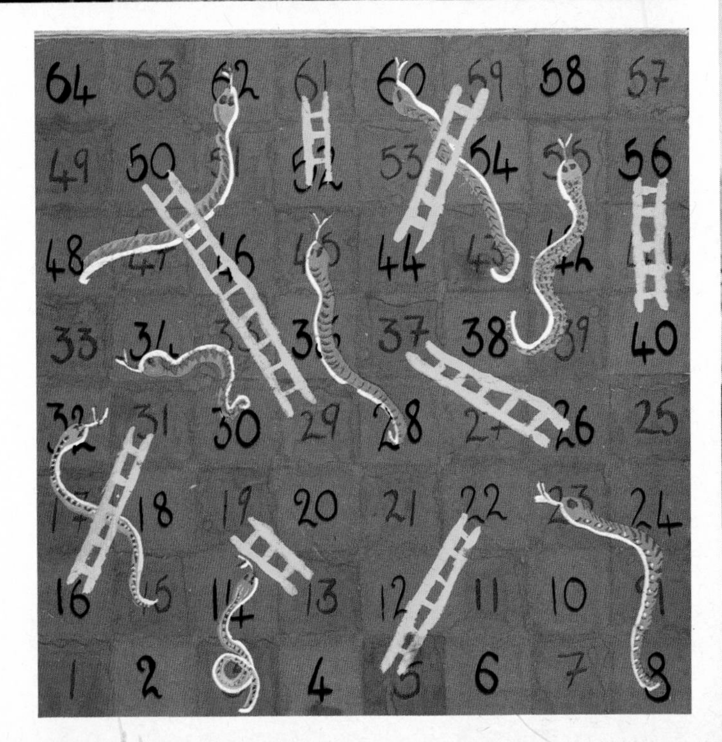

Credits List

Aldus Archives 95(TR) (BR), 120(B), 127, 136(T), 146(B), 149(TR), 155(TR), 158(T); © Aldus Books, (Rudolph Britto) 66(TL), 87(B), 93(B), 94(B), 149(B), (Photo Mike Busselle) 77(B), (Photo Ken Coton) 88(BR), (Photo Geoffrey Drury) 13(B), (Photo John Freeman) 114, (Anna Lovell) 157(B), (Edward Powers) 51, 85(T); Archiv für Kunst und Geschichte, Berlin 136(B); Archives Photographiques, Paris 86(T); Archivs der Stadt- und Universitätsbibliothek, Frankfurt am Main 140(T); Associated Press photos (Musée de Arte Sacro de la Catédrale de Evora, Portugal) 62–63(TC); 79(B); Barnabys 96(B), 157(T); Bettmann Archive Inc. 143(T) (C); Biblioteca Apostolica Vaticana 54–55(B), 98(T); Bibliothèque Nationale, Paris 19(T), 61(TR), 103(BL), 107(BR), 109, 128; Bodleian Library, Oxford 42(TR), 93(T), 105(TL); Bollingen Foundation/Photos Fred Anderegg 41(B), 98–99(B); British Crown Copyright 56(T); By permission of the Trustees of the British Museum 10(T), 12(B), 43(B), 58(B), 88(TR), 89(B), 102, 105(TR), 108(B), 113(BR), 122(B), 125(B); British Museum (Photos © Aldus Books) Brompton Studios 18, John Freeman 12(TL), 21(L), 73(B), 120(T), 126(B), 132(B), R.L. Jarmain 96(T), John Webb 97(B), David Swann 15; Courtesy of The Brooklyn Museum, Charles E. Wilbour Collection 10(B); Bruckmann Bildarchiv München 92(T); Photo Russ Busby 81(B); Caligari Archive 66(B), 113(T), 117(B), 118(TR) (BR), 123(B), 124(BL), 137(T), 139(B); From Russell and Whitehead, *Principia Mathematica*, Cambridge University Press, London, 1910 148(T); From Ulli Beier, *African Mud Sculpture*, Cambridge University Press, London, 1963 75(T); Photo J. Allan Cash 151(T); Courtesy the Governing Body of Christ Church, Oxford 122(T); © 1910 renewed 1938 The Christian Science Publishing Society. All rights reserved. 77(T3rdR); The Danish National Museum, Copenhagen 8(T); Photo Rosemary Davies 58(T); From Edward Muybridge, *Animals in Motion*, Dover Publications, Inc., New York, 1957 142–143(B); Euan Duff 85(B), 159(BR); Edinburgh National Gallery 126(T); Edinburgh University Library 39(B), 56(B); Editions Cercle d'Art, Paris 43(T); Photo Wim Swaan from Enrique Sordo, *Moorish Spain*, Paul Elek Productions Ltd., London 59(BR); Fritz Eschen 155(TL); Photo Tony Evans 29(T); Les Films Fernand Rivers, S.A. 154; Photo by courtesy of the French Government Tourist Office, London 42(L); Reproduced by permission of the Syndics of the Fitzwilliam Museum, Cambridge 105(B); Friends Meeting House/Photo Roger Hyde © Aldus Books 70(T); From Hermann Zeltner, *Schelling*, Frommans Klassiker der Philosophie XXXIII, Friedrich Frommann Verlag, Stuttgart 135(B); Photo Georg Gerster 52(B); Photo Emil Gmelin, Dornach 77(T4thR); Gräfe und Unzer Verlag, München 132(T); Photos Sonia Halliday 48(TL), 49(BR); Philippe Halsman 81(TL); Stephen Harrison 53(B), 57(B), 59(BL), 63(TR), 74(T), 75(B); André Held, Lausanne 19(B), 69(B); Archives Verlag Herder Freiburg 100; Hamburger Kunsthalle/Photo Ralph Kleinhempel 130; Photos Michael Holford 8(B), 9(TR), 14(BR), 62; Holle Bildarchiv, Baden-Baden 28(B); From J. Doresse, *The Secret Books of the Egyptian Gnostics*, Hollis & Carter Ltd., London 103(TL); Hungarian Academy of Sciences, Kaufmann Collection/Photo Behram Kapadia © Aldus Books 108(TL); Hunting Surveys Limited 95(TL); Imperial College of Science and Technology, London 147(T); Isotope Institute Ltd., London 152; Jewish Institute of History, Warsaw 45(T); Keystone 36(BR), 76(T), 79(L), 133, 148(B), 151(B); Landesmuseum, Trier 121(B); From Martin Lawrence, *The Land Without Unemployment*, Lawrence & Wishart Ltd., London, 1931 137(B); © Stefan Lochner, München 141(B); Magnum Photos (Brian Brake) 32(BR), (Rene Burri) 36(BL), (Charles Harbutt) 45(B), (Erich Lessing) 117(T), (Inge Morath) 63(BR), (Marilyn Silverstone) 30(B); Felix H. Mann 155(BL); Mansell Collection 20, 23(T), 38(T) (B), 72(B), 78(T), 84(3B), 89(T), 103(BR), 107(L), 111, 112(T), 116, 121(L), 129, 135(T), 138; Courtesy Lincoln Laboratory, Massachusetts Institute of Technology 153(T); Photos Roger Mayne 158(BR), 159(BL); Albin Michel 144; Photo W.T. Miller 11(B); Monumenti Musei e Gallerie Pontificie, Vatican 94(T); Musée Condé de Chantilly/Photo Giraudon 72(T); Photo Musée d'Aquitaine, Bordeaux 14(BL); Musée de Versailles 119; Musée du Louvre, Paris/Photos Giraudon 16(B), 17(T); Musée Guimet 27(B), (Photo J.A. Lavaud) 74(B); Courtesy, Museum of Fine Arts, Boston. Fenollosa-Weld Collection 34(T); The National Gallery, London 118(L); National Portrait Gallery, London 70(CL), 73(T), 124(BR), 139(T); Nietzsche Archiv, Weimar 141(T); Ada and Emil Nolde Foundation, Seebull 147(B); Bildarchiv der Österreichischen Nationalbibliothek Wien 153(BR); Bavaria-Verlag, PAF International 13(T), 30(T), 48(BL)(TR), 49(TR), 50(BL), 57(T), 80(B); David Paramor Collection, London 34(B), 77(TL), 142(T); Picturepoint, London 59(T); 61(TL), 150(B), 159(T); Photo Rosemarie Pierer 52(T); Popperfotos 9(B), 30(C), 97(T); Photos Sandra Prato 24, 32(T); From Otto Fischer, *Die Kunst Indiens, Chinas und Japans*, Propyläen Verlag, Berlin, 1928, 35(L); Radio Times Hulton Picture Library 68(T), 77(T2ndR), 78(B), 140(B), 149(TC); Günter R. Reitz, Hannover 16(T); From L. Wittgenstein (trans. C.K. Ogden), *Tractatus Logico-Philosophicus*, Routledge & Kegan Paul Ltd., London and Humanities Press, New York 156; From Daisetz T. Suzuki, *Zen and Japanese Culture*, Routledge & Kegan Paul Ltd., London, 1952 36(TL); Rijksmuseum, Amsterdam 67(T); Jean Rowntree 84(T); The Royal Society 146(T); Sassoon Library, Letchworth/Photo David Swann © Aldus Books 40(B); Photos Scala, Florence 2, 14(T), 23(B), 27(TR), 46, 49(TL), 50(T) (BR), 53(T), 68(B), 69(T), 71, 82, 86(B), 90(T), 104, 106(T); Photo Edwin Smith 21(TR); Vernon Sproxton 81(BL); Staatliche Museen Preuss. Kulturbesitz, Frühchristliche-Byzantinische Sammlung, Berlin 103(TR); Staatliche Museen, Stiftung Preussischer Kulturbesitz, Berlin 17(B), 91(B); Photo Shabtai Tal 44; The Tate Gallery, London/Photo John Freeman © Aldus Books 134; Three Lions, Inc. 26(TR), 27(TL), 28(T), 29(B), 31(T) (B), 36(CR), 41(T), 67(B), 76(B), 80(T) (B); Courtesy The Board of Trinity College, Dublin 60(T); Emily Underwood 158(BL); United States Information Service, London 64; United States Travel Service 150(TL); By permission of the Syndics of the University Library, Cambridge 87(T), 106(B), 112(B); Department of Philosophy, Philosopher Portrait Collection, University of California, Los Angeles 153(BL); Noud van den Eerenbeemt 35(TR); By courtesy of the Victoria & Albert Museum, London/(Photo John Freeman © Aldus Books) 6, (Photo David Swann © Aldus Books) 26(B); From George Boole, *Studies in Logic and Probability*, C.A. Watts & Co. Ltd., London, 1952 149(TL); Photo Reg Wilson 158(CL); Photo Gino Zangheri 108(TR); Zemaljski muzej, Sarajevo 40(T); Zentrale Farbbild Agentur GmbH., Düsseldorf 33, 37, 55(T)

Below: to all appearances, some of these engine controls are similar, yet each one has a separate function; and unless that function is clearly understood it is impossible to make the engine work efficiently. In the same way, words must be used with a clear understanding of their use to allow successful communication.